THE
UNLIKELY
REFORMER

Carter Glass was an architect of the modern regulatory state—a principal author of the Federal Reserve Act, the Glass-Steagall Act, and of important provisions of the Securities Exchange Act. Yet who in the public remembers this fiery, diminutive and irascible son of the Old South? Raised in post-Civil War Virginia, Glass's political roots lay deep in the Jim Crow ideology of white supremacy. He was so set in his ways that he practically refused to ride in an automobile. Yet, while never transcending the ideology of segregation, Glass transformed himself from small-time Congressman to a power in the Senate with national standing, a populist champion of financial reform and regulation. Few American legislators had more enduring influence than the one-time newspaperman whose political career lasted from the Gilded Age through the New Deal, At long last, Matthew Fink brings us the biography we have been waiting for. Fink gives us a rollicking ride with one of the most improbable—and colorful—American politicians of the Twentieth Century. With financial reform—and Glass-Steagall itself—still on the table *The Unlikely Reformer* could not be more timely, or more fun.

Roger Lowenstein, Author,
America's Bank: The Epic Struggle to Create the Federal Reserve

THE UNLIKELY REFORMER

Carter Glass and Financial Regulation

By Matthew P. Fink

George Mason University Press

Fairfax, Virginia

THE UNLIKELY REFORMER
Carter Glass and
Financial Regulation
By Matthew P. Fink

George Mason University Press
Fairfax, Virginia

Copyright © 2019 by George Mason University Press

ISBN: 978-1-942695-16-5 (trade paper)
ISBN: 978-1-942695-17-2 (ebook)

First edition.

Library of Congress Cataloging-in-Publication Data forthcoming.

Printed in the United States of America

Designed by Emily L. Cole

Cover image: "The Coming Money Trust,"
Alfred Owen Crozier, *U.S. Money vs. Corporation Currency*, 1912.

To: Emily, Nina, and Owen

Table of Contents

Images

Credits appear with images.

INTRODUCTION

Carter Glass is the single most important
lawmaker in the history of American finance.

—Richard E. Farley

The 2008 financial crisis has caused policy makers, historians, and journalists to examine previous financial crises and government responses to them. In particular, they have looked back to the two major financial crises of the last century, the Panic of 1907 and the 1929 crash, and to the laws passed in reaction to those traumatic events.

The Panic of 1907 led to the enactment of the Federal Reserve Act of 1913, often described as the most important financial law in U.S. history since it created a mechanism to manage the nation's currency and address panics. The principal author of the act was a virtually unknown middle-aged Democratic congressman from Virginia, Carter Glass. Glass had little experience in banking and finance. His main political act prior to 1913 was placing provisions in the Virginia constitution that severely limited voting by black citizens. He reached a position of power in the House of Representatives through the prevailing seniority system.

The next serious financial crisis was the 1929 crash. It was followed by the Great Depression and the election of Franklin Roosevelt as president. During Roosevelt's first two terms, Congress enacted a long series of major economic and financial laws, including the Agricultural Adjustment Act, the Fair Labor Standards Act, the National Industrial Recovery Act, the National Labor Relations

Act, the Public Utility Holding Company Act, the Securities Act, the Securities Exchange Act, the Social Security Act, and the Tennessee Valley Development Act.

Initially, almost all members of Congress supported New Deal laws. Over time, New Deal measures faced increasing opposition from most Republicans and from some southern Democrats. Glass, now a senator from Virginia, was an early Democrat opponent of most of the New Deal. Glass developed the strongest anti–New Deal record of any Democratic senator: "His record of opposition to the New Deal, based on a study of thirty-one bills on which he voted, 1933–1939, was 81 percent opposed—easily the highest of all Democratic senators of the period."[1] In 1937, Glass vehemently opposed FDR's unsuccessful plan to pack the Supreme Court. In 1940, Glass fought against Roosevelt's successful bid for nomination to an unprecedented third term. Glass had the well-deserved reputation of being the most vociferous Democratic opponent of the New Deal.

Yet Glass was the principal author of one of the major laws passed in the First Hundred Days of the New Deal, the Glass-Steagall Act, which placed controls on bank lending for securities speculation, prohibited banks from directly engaging in securities activities, barred banks from being affiliated with securities firms, and provided for federal insurance of bank deposits. Glass also authored provisions in the Securities Exchange Act of 1934, which created the United States Securities and Exchange Commission (the SEC), often viewed as the model New Deal agency.

In short, Carter Glass, usually pictured as an anti-government southern reactionary, was responsible for some of the most progressive and important financial legislation in American history—the Federal Reserve Act, the Glass-Steagall Act, and provisions of the Securities Exchange Act creating the SEC.

Glass's legislative accomplishments were widely recognized during his lifetime. In 1918, five years after the enactment of the Federal Reserve Act, President Wilson appointed Glass Secretary of the

Treasury. In 1929 after the Great Crash, in a highly unusual move, the Republican-controlled Senate named Glass, a Democrat, to chair a subcommittee to look into banking reform legislation, which resulted in the Glass-Steagall Act of 1933. After enactment of that act, President Roosevelt offered to name Glass Secretary of the Treasury for the second time. The two major biographies of Glass were published in 1938 and 1939.[2]

By contrast, in more recent years little attention has been paid to Glass. Countless books and articles have been written about legislation and regulation during the Wilson Administration, the 1920s, and the New Deal. Many of these works discuss one or two matters in which Glass was involved. However, there is no book or article that covers *all* of the many financial regulatory matters in which Glass played a critical role or that discusses why Glass took the positions that he did. This book is the first work that explores, in detail, Glass's approach to financial regulation during his remarkable 43-year career as a congressman, Secretary of the Treasury, and senator.

Glass's political views reflected his upbringing in Lynchburg, Virginia, the heart of the old South, immediately after the Civil War. Glass's hero was an earlier Virginian, Thomas Jefferson. At the very beginning of the nation, Secretary of State Jefferson had opposed an activist federal government since he feared it would favor financiers and merchants at the expense of farmers. Instead, Jefferson supported states' rights and localism. Glass was convinced that Jefferson was the greatest statesman the United States had ever produced and adopted Jefferson's antagonism to an activist federal government and northern financial interests. Glass's Jeffersonian beliefs were strengthened by his view of Reconstruction, the political program that the federal government imposed on the South after the Civil War. Reconstruction provided former slaves with basic civil rights, notably voting rights, and deprived Confederate office holders and military officers of the rights to vote and hold office. Glass was an avowed anti-black racist and regarded Reconstruction as an attempt to destroy the white civilization of the South. As a newspaper publisher, Glass wrote editorials criticizing black civil rights and Wall Street. He then became active in Virginia politics, with his crowning racist achievement being provisions in the state's new constitution depriving most blacks of the right to vote.

During his four decades in national politics, Glass opposed most reform measures since they would have greatly expanded federal power. Glass was willing to make exceptions for reform legislation aimed at his other bête noire, northern financial interests. However, even here Glass supported legislative approaches that sought to curb private financial power by fragmenting that power rather than by providing the federal government with new authority. Thus, following the Panic of 1907, Glass opposed legislation that would have created a single all-powerful central bank. Instead, he authored the Federal Reserve Act of 1913, which provided for a decentralized system consisting of a number of regional reserve banks in cities across the nation. After the 1929 crash, there were proposals to regulate security activities conducted by investment firms that were controlled by commercial banks. Instead, Glass authored the Glass-Steagall Act of 1933, which fragmented the nation's financial system by separating commercial and investment banking. At times, Glass also pursued a fragmentation approach with respect to government itself. In 1934, he succeeded in placing federal regulation of the securities markets in a new specialized federal agency, the Securities and Exchange Commission, rather than in a large existing agency with other responsibilities, the Federal Trade Commission.

Glass exhibited great tenacity and skill in getting his fragmentation proposals enacted into law. As soon as Glass was appointed to the House Banking Committee in 1903, he undertook an in-depth study of banking issues. Therefore, even before Woodrow Wilson was elected president in 1912, Glass was able to prepare legislation that became the Federal Reserve Act. Similarly, before Franklin Roosevelt was elected president in 1932, Glass, then a senator, developed banking reform legislation that became the Glass-Steagall Act. Glass combined technical mastery of complex banking issues, political acumen, and fierce determination to achieve a series of legislative victories in the financial area.

Glass was helped by the fact that many of his political contemporaries were personally fond of him and his idiosyncrasies. Glass was an ill-tempered curmudgeon who hated the modern age. He distrusted those new-fangled conveyances, automobiles; opposed the change in Senate offices from operator-run phones to dial phones; and moved out of his hotel after twenty-five years when the lobby was remodeled. In 1935, Glass summed up his general attitude, "now is about as good a time as anybody could find to die, when the country is being taken to hell as fast as a lot of miseducated fools can get it there." Vice President Garner stated, "No one can help but like that old rooster," and most famously, President Franklin Roosevelt named Glass an "Unreconstructed Rebel."[3] A photograph of Glass and Roosevelt on page 130 bears the inscription, "For Carter from Franklin D. Roosevelt. Both Unreconstructed Rebels and proud of it."

Over the decades, changes have been made to the Federal Reserve Act, the Glass-Steagall Act, and the Securities Exchange Act. However, today they still constitute the foundation of the American financial system. The Federal Reserve Act continues to provide for a unique geographically decentralized reserve banking system to manage the nation's currency and address panics. The Securities Exchange Act still requires that American securities markets (expanded in 1940 to include investment companies and investment advisers) be regulated by the same independent federal agency, the SEC. The greatest change has occurred in the Glass-Steagall Act, where in 1999 Congress repealed provisions separating banks and securities firms. Provisions limiting commercial bank lending for securities speculation, creating a system of federal deposit insurance, prohibiting direct bank involvement in securities activities, and barring securities firms from taking deposits, however, remain in place. Thus, almost all of

Glass's core legislative accomplishments still serve as the key building blocks of the American financial system.

1
GLASS'S FORMATIVE YEARS IN VIRGINIA

His Virginian distaste for being ruled from afar found
a central bank in Wall Street or a Treasury bureau
in Washington equally repellent.

—Gerald T. Dunne

Glass grew up in Virginia in the wake of the Civil War. He was poor, self-educated, and self-made, rising from newspaper delivery boy to newspaper owner. He was committed to the Democratic Party and white supremacy, and was fearful of outsiders, including the federal government and Northern financial interests. His success in amending the Virginia constitution to deprive black citizens of the vote made his political reputation and led to his election to Congress in 1902.

Glass's Background

Glass came from modest circumstances. He was born in 1858 in Lynchburg, Virginia, a city of approximately 7,000 people located east of the Blue Ridge Mountains. Both of his parents came from families that had lived in Virginia for generations. He was one of twelve children. His mother died when he was two, and he was raised by an older sister. Glass's father, Robert Glass, was first the editor and

1. Glass as a Baby and Age 14. First appeared in *Carter Glass: Unreconstructed Rebel*, James E. Palmer, Jr., 1938.

then the owner of a newspaper. He also was appointed postmaster. He fought for the Confederacy in the Civil War, earning the title "Major Glass." After the war, Major Glass refused a reappointment as postmaster because of his intense dislike of the federal government he had just fought against. Major Glass considered entering politics, but Reconstruction, with the Virginia government run by Republicans and the disenfranchisement of ex-Confederates, made that impossible. Carter Glass recalled evenings when his family went to bed hungry.[1]

Glass was tiny and frail, growing to a height of only five feet, four inches tall and weighing less than one hundred pounds. As a boy, he was feisty and combative. He was willing to take on bigger boys physically, earning the nickname "Pluck." He left public school at age fourteen because of his family's difficult economic circumstances. He was largely self-educated, reading classics such as Plato, Shakespeare, and Edmund Burke.

Glass followed his father into the newspaper business. His business career was a classic self-made success story. He advanced from being a newspaper delivery boy to printer's devil (apprentice) to reporter to editor to publisher. In 1888, the owner of the *Lynchburg News*, Albert Waddill, wanted to retire and to sell the paper to Glass, then editor-in chief, who borrowed funds and purchased the paper. When Waddill announced the sale, he went out of his way to praise Glass, "I am ... much gratified that the ownership of the paper has fallen to one, who, while as yet a very young man, has achieved an enviable name for character, capacity, and indomitable energy."[2]

Glass proved to be an extremely successful publisher of the *Lynchburg News*. He lowered the paper's price, and circulation sky-rocketed. Glass used increased revenues from subscriptions and advertisements to pay off the debt he had taken on to purchase the paper. In 1893, he acquired the competing morning paper and merged it into the *News*. In 1895, he acquired the sole evening paper and thus obtained a newspaper monopoly in the Lynchburg area.[3]

Glass's editorials covered a wide range of topics that went well beyond matters involving Lynchburg and Virginia, such as the Boulanger Affair in France, Matthew Arnold's criticisms of America, and the debate over who wrote Shakespeare's plays. Glass's editorials reflected wide reading, critical thinking, and the ability to transmit his thoughts to others.

Glass's Political Views

Glass's political hero was an earlier Virginian and one of the nation's founding fathers, Thomas Jefferson. At the very beginning of the Republic, Secretary of State Jefferson had opposed a broad interpretation of the federal government's authority and instead favored a limited federal government, states' rights, and localism. This was exemplified by Jefferson's unsuccessful battle against Secretary of the Treasury Alexander Hamilton's proposal to create the First Bank of the United States, which would issue currency, act as the government's agent in collecting taxes, and make loans. Jefferson feared that such a bank inevitably would favor financiers and merchants over farmers. Jefferson founded what became the Democratic Party in order to have a political organization that could espouse and implement his views.

Glass was convinced that Jefferson was "the wisest man of his period and had the most fertile mind of any person who had lived before him or who has lived since."[4] Glass adopted Jefferson's distrust of both federal authority and powerful northern financial interests, and was a fervent supporter of the Democratic Party.

Glass's Jeffersonian beliefs were reinforced by his views of three developments that occurred during his lifetime—the Civil War, Reconstruction of the South after the war, and the creation of the Readjuster Party in Virginia.

Glass was born in 1858 and so was a child during the Civil War, which raged from 1861 to 1865. Glass had distinct memories of

2. Glass as a Young Newspaper Publisher and His Family. First appeared in
Carter Glass: Unreconstructed Rebel, James E. Palmer, Jr., 1938.

Confederate soldiers marching off to war and of hearing rifle shots from North-South skirmishes outside of Lynchburg.[5] Glass also remembered his encounter with a troop of Union cavalry shortly after the war ended. He refused to get out of the road as the troop came toward him. A Union officer lifted Glass up onto his saddle and asked what the boy was going to do when he grew up. Glass replied, "A major, like my father, and shoot Yankees."[6]

The Civil War was followed by the period of Reconstruction from 1865 to 1877, when the federal government sought to impose a totally new political structure on the Southern states. Former black slaves were given the right to vote and other civil rights. Conversely, former Confederate officeholders and military officers were prohibited from holding public office and voting. Federal troops were stationed in the South to enforce the new political order. Two of Glass's early biographers set forth Glass's racist view regarding Reconstruction in Virginia:

> Under protection of soldiers a locust swarm of carpetbaggers [northern opportunists] descended upon Virginia ... and through the Negro voters radicals were in complete control. Practically all Virginians of any experience were disfranchised and disqualified from holding public office. It was not long before Negro radicals were surpassing even their white leaders in exorbitant demands ... a short while longer and Negroes were drawing the color line themselves.[7]

Glass's hatred of Reconstruction, with the federal government granting voting and other civil rights to black Americans, continued throughout has life. In 1937, when Glass opposed President Franklin Roosevelt's plan to pack the Supreme Court, he defended the court since it had "validated the [anti-black] suffrage laws of the South which saved the section from anarchy and ruin in a period

3. Glass About the Time He First Went to Washington. First appeared in *Carter Glass: A Biography*, Rixey Smith and Norman Beasley, 1939.

[of Reconstruction] the unspeakable outrages of which nearly all the Nation recalls with shame."[8] Glass's detestation of Reconstruction strengthened his devotion to the Democratic Party since it opposed an activist federal government, particularly one which worked for civil rights for black Americans. In 1888, when Glass became owner of the *Lynchburg News,* he reaffirmed his devotion to Lynchburg and "my unswerving attachment to the principles and policies on the Democratic party."[9] In 1935, when a correspondent asked why Glass was so loyal to the party, Glass replied that "the unspeakable atrocities of the reconstruction era made every white man regard his party allegiance even more important than his religion, since it involved the very preservation of Anglo-Saxon liberty."[10]

When Glass described Reconstruction with phrases such as "anarchy and ruin," "unspeakable outrages," and "unspeakable atrocities," he was not referring to murder, rape, or similar abuses, but merely to granting black Americans the right to vote. An 1889 editorial Glass wrote conveyed the degree to which white supremacy and civilization were entangled in his thinking:

> Those who treat the question of race supremacy with an air of flippancy ... do not do not seem to comprehend that it is with no animosity toward the negro race that the white people of this section insist upon their exclusion from the administration of the State governments. Apparently they cannot conceive, what is manifest to us, that the dominion of the blacks in municipal or State affairs would be incompatible with the public safety and, indeed, fatal to a high order of civilization."

After Reconstruction ended in 1877, white Democrats reassumed control of the Virginia government. In 1879, a coalition of Republicans, white farmers, and working men, many of whom had been Democrats, and black farmers and working men founded the Readjuster Party. The party's main goal was to reduce the principal and interest owed on the state's pre–Civil War debt, so that the state could spend more on public schools. The party also promised to repeal the poll tax, which made it difficult for blacks to vote. The Readjuster Party was led by William Mahone, who had been a Confederate general in the Civil War and a railroad executive. The Readjuster Party captured both houses of the Virginia legislature, which enacted legislation reducing principal and interest on the state debt. The Readjuster Party, with its biracial constituency and commitment to reducing the state's obligations in order to fund public institutions, was anathema to Glass. He used the *Lynchburg News* to launch a vitriolic racial attack on the party and Mahone, calling him "the wily leader of the mongrel party."[12] Because of Glass's attacks, Mahone lost a race for Governor running as a Republican in 1889. Mahone largely retired from politics. The episode enhanced Glass's reputation for audacity, a sharp tongue, and devotion to the Democratic Party and white supremacy.

Glass regularly commented on national issues, including the long-running battle during the 1880s and 1890s over the nation's currency. Conservatives, large banks, and business generally favored continuation of currency backed by gold since they believed that this would help the dollar retain its purchasing power. Agrarians in the South and West wanted currency to be backed by silver in addition to gold since they believed that this would expand the money supply and make it easier for them to obtain credit.

Virginia was firmly in the agrarian camp. Its farmers had faced severe economic hardship since the end of the Civil War. The wholesale price index for Virginia commodities fell from 189.7 in 1865 to 85.2 in 1885. The tobacco farmers in Glass's own area were particularly hard hit.[13] Virginia farmers attributed their poor economic condition to a vast conspiracy that was headed by "the bankers, speculators, and monopolists of Wall Street. In the 1890s gold became a symbol of this imagined plot, and currency reform [backing currency with silver as well as gold] grew into the great issue of the day."[14]

Glass strongly favored the silver approach and was vitriolic in his criticism of supporters of the gold standard, particularly Wall Street. In 1893, Glass declared: "Gold is Wall Street's only god and those who don't bow down and worship it have no business in that quarter."[15]

Glass was pleased when a panic hit Wall Street, declaring: "If it shall prove to be a genuine cyclone and wipe out all of the speculative rottenness that pervades that gambling den the atmosphere would be much purer and the people in the country could breathe much freer than for several years."[16] In 1894, when President Cleveland obtained repeal of an act providing for government purchases of silver, Glass wrote: "It is just the money power that the old United

States Biddle bank used to exercise over the finances of the government and country, and would exercise this day had not General Jackson in his might crushed out its last charter."[17]

These editorials were examples of Glass's tendency to see political and economic issues in moral terms and to view his opponents as evil conspirators. "Even the issue of free silver was for him as much a moral problem as a financial one. Without understanding the intricacies of finance, he convinced himself that a vast conspiracy for the gold standard emanated from Wall and Lombard Streets, masterminded by the creditor interests which benefitted from an appreciating currency."[18]

Glass's Start in Politics

Given Glass's reputation as a successful businessman and commentator on public affairs, it is not surprising that he became active in politics. In 1883, he was appointed clerk of the Lynchburg City Council, where he became familiar with legal phraseology and the state's auditing of county and city accounts. He was a delegate to the National Democratic Conventions in 1892 and 1896. At the 1896 convention, he supported William Jennings Bryan's calls for the monetization of silver. Glass subsequently disowned this populist approach, attributing his earlier position to his almost complete ignorance of monetary theory at that time.[19]

In 1901, Glass served as a delegate to a convention that was called to design a new constitution for Virginia. The major issue involved limiting voting by black citizens. One group of delegates wanted to eliminate every possible black voter. Another group wanted to protect the voting rights of every white. Glass successfully pushed for a middle-ground approach, one that would disenfranchise the vast majority of blacks as well as some whites. Glass did this through imposition of both a poll tax and an "understanding clause" that required black citizens to demonstrate to white election officials their understanding of constitutional questions. Two observers concluded that Glass had succeeded in achieving his odious goal: "The colored vote had been reduced to 25,000. Today, out of the 25,000 potential colored voters in Richmond, for example, there are only about 1,800 Negroes eligible to vote under Virginia restrictions."[20]

Glass's success at the 1901 Virginia constitutional convention made his political reputation. He had become "an important figure in the eyes of many Virginians. He had proven himself not only a serious-minded senator but, under pressure, a keen and intelligent debater."[21]

Shortly after the convention, Glass sought the Democratic nomination for a seat in the United States House of Representatives. He won both the nomination and the subsequent election.

2
GLASS GOES TO WASHINGTON: REPUBLICANS FAIL TO ENACT BANKING LEGISLATION

You never want a serious crisis to go to waste.

—Rahm Emanuel

When Glass entered the House in 1903, the nation lacked a mechanism for managing the currency and addressing panics. Bankers and businessmen offered legislative proposals, but the Republican-controlled Congress and Republican President Theodore Roosevelt were not interested in banking legislation. Following the Panic of 1907, Republican Senator Aldrich proposed a plan providing for a centralized reserve banking system controlled by private banks. The Aldrich Plan was not submitted to Congress until early 1912, by which time Congress was controlled by Democrats, who opposed the plan.

Glass Enters the House of Representatives

When Glass took his seat as a Democrat in the House of Representatives in March 1903, the Republicans controlled the federal government. Republican Theodore Roosevelt occupied the White House. The Republicans held a 57 to 33 majority in the Senate and a 210 to 176 majority in the House. The Republicans had controlled the federal government since 1897, and it appeared that it would be a long time, if ever, before the Democrats would displace them. Moreover, the Republicans in turn were controlled by a small group—the president and a few members of Congress.[1]

Despite these facts, Glass likely would have felt at home in the House because the Democratic minority was dominated by southerners. Over half (96) of the Democratic representatives came from the eleven former Confederate states. Twenty-eight other Congressmen were from the border states of Delaware, Kentucky, Maryland, and Missouri. Most Democratic leadership positions were held by representatives from the southern and border states.

Initially, Glass was a quiet member of the House. He did not make a speech on the floor until his third term, and that speech was delivered in memory of a colleague. Glass sought a seat on the Committee on Foreign Affairs, but he was first assigned to the Committee on Public Lands, and then to the Committee on Banking and Currency. That committee was a quiet backwater since there were no major banking and currency issues before Congress. Moreover, since the Republicans had an overwhelming majority in the House, Glass and his fellow Democrats had little influence. Nevertheless, Glass evidenced the same diligence that he had demonstrated during his business career. From the time he was appointed to the House Banking Committee, Glass steeped himself on banking issues.

> He read hundreds of books on banking and finance. He interviewed everybody available whose opinion seemed worthwhile. He asked questions. He visited banks of all types and sizes—small-town banks in Virginia and large institutions in New York City. He interviewed small merchants and great industrialists as to their financial needs. He studied monetary systems and the history of money, even the systems of the Aztecs.[2]

The Banking Situation in 1903

When Glass entered the House, the United States lacked a central bank that provided a means of managing the nation's currency and addressing financial panics. The country had had experience with *elements* of a central bank. In 1791, Congress established the First Bank of the United States. While it did not function like a modern central bank, which regulates commercial banks, holds their reserves, and acts as a lender of last resort, it could alter the supply of money and credit in the economy. Its charter expired in 1811. In 1816, Congress established the Second Bank of the United States. President Andrew Jackson vetoed its re-chartering in 1836. There were no further efforts to create a full or even partial central bank.

In 1900, U.S. currency consisted of a mixture of greenbacks issued during the Civil War, treasury notes of 1890, and, most important, bank notes issued by national banks and secured by U.S. government bonds. Many bankers and businessmen believed that this existing bond-secured currency was too "inelastic." By this, they meant that the amount of currency in circulation did not expand sufficiently when needed. For example, the stock of currency did not increase when farmers needed more funds in the spring when they planted crops or in the fall when they needed more funds to harvest crops. During financial panics many people wanted to convert their bank deposits into currency. However, there was no mechanism for temporarily increasing the amount of currency in circulation to meet this irregular demand.[3]

Bankers and businessmen proposed several solutions to address the problem of currency inelasticity. The most common proposal was to permit national banks to secure additional bank notes with their general assets—such as commercial paper, railroad bonds, and state and local government bonds—beyond the volume of notes strictly supported by U.S. government bonds. This approach was reflected in a number of differing proposals made in 1894 by bankers of the Baltimore Clearing House, Secretary of the Treasury John G.

Carlisle, and Comptroller of the Currency James H. Eckels; in 1898 by businessmen in the form of the Indianapolis Monetary Commission; and in 1906 by the New York Chamber of Commerce and Currency Commission of the American Bankers Association.[4]

In addition to the problem of currency inelasticity, there was no mechanism in place for tying together the thousands of commercial banks that existed across the nation. There were state-chartered banks in each of the states. There were national banks chartered by the federal government. State and national banks operated side-by-side in a dual system with differing rules. State laws prohibited state and national banks from operating branches, which meant that there were a large number of banks that had just one office. As a result of this fragmentation, by 1913 there were almost 30,000 banks in the country.[5] The only connection among banks was the local clearinghouses located in major cities that facilitated transactions among banks within that geographic region. Historian Frederick Lewis Allen wrote that "the individual banks were so independent of one another that there was no way of mobilizing their scattered reserves to meet emergencies in one part of the country or another. Each bank had to sink or swim by itself, aided only by such relief measures as a local clearinghouse could contrive or some local leader could impose upon the local banks."[6]

There were numerous proposals to ameliorate the lack of coordination among banks, such as having the federal government create *national* clearinghouses with the power to issue currency; permitting branch banking; and establishing a strong central bank. Paul M. Warburg, a partner of Kuhn, Loeb & Company, a prominent investment bank, called for following the European model, which used a strong central bank and an elastic currency backed primarily by commercial paper issued by business enterprises.[7] No two proposals were the same. Each element of each proposal had advocates and opponents within the banking industry. Moreover, while some bankers favored reform, most bankers were not sufficiently concerned to push for

Congressional legislation.

Key political leaders did not evidence much interest in banking reform legislation. Senator Nelson W. Aldrich, chairman of the Senate Finance Committee and arguably the most influential Republican member of Congress, was content with the status quo. President Theodore Roosevelt found banking issues too technical and boring to attract his attention.[8] In the absence of a crisis, with bankers generally passive, and without presidential leadership, Congress did not take any serious action regarding banking issues.

The Panic of 1907

In January 1906, Jacob H. Schiff, head of Kuhn, Loeb & Company, gave a speech to the New York Chamber of Commerce in which he warned that "during the past sixty days, conditions in the New York money market ... are nothing less than a disgrace to a civilized country," and "if this condition of affairs is not changed, and changed soon, we will get a panic in this country compared with which those which have preceded it will look like child's play."[9] Schiff's prophecy soon came true.

The year 1907 was marked by an unusually high demand for money. The problem was exacerbated by the 1906 San Francisco earthquake, which resulted in large payments by insurance companies that had to raise the funds by liquidating investments and withdrawing deposits; by movements in interest rates; and by falling stock prices. Business confidence was further eroded by President Theodore Roosevelt's speech attacking "malefactors of great wealth."[10]

There also was a persistent structural weakness in the banking system in the nation's financial capital, New York City. A new type of institution, the state-chartered trust company, had emerged in the late nineteenth century to handle wills, estates, and corporate trust matters. Over time, they took on more and more of the powers of traditional commercial banks, such as accepting deposits and making commercial loans. However, trust companies were subject to far less stringent regulation than commercial banks. For example, trust companies were required to maintain reserves at far lower levels than commercial banks. This permitted trust companies to pay higher interest rates to attract deposits than commercial banks could normally afford. As a result, deposit money poured into trust companies and their assets grew at a far greater rate than bank assets. "In 1906, the assets of all trust companies in New York City, approximated the assets of all national banks, and exceeded the assets of all state banks."[11] There were proposals to subject trust companies to the same rules that applied to commercial banks, but in the absence of a crisis, trust companies successfully resisted these efforts.

The Panic of 1907 began when Fritz Augustus Heinze, a mining engineer, his brother, Otto, and Charles W. Morse, who controlled several banks, sought to corner the market in shares of United Copper Company. When the attempt was unsuccessful, the brokerage firm the group had used failed. The public worried that the group's failure in the stock market also threatened the group's commercial banks.

> Heinze was president of the Mercantile National Bank; Morse and Thomas were directors of it. When the Heinze [stock market] failure was headlined on the front pages of the papers, depositors naturally became suspicious and began to withdraw their funds. Suspicion spread to the Morse chain of banks, too. The Mercantile, finding its cash being drained away by uneasy depositors, applied to the Clearing House for help.[12]

A series of dominoes fell: first, the brokerage firm used to effect the corner, then two banks owned by Morse, next a Montana savings bank owned by Augustus Heinze that acted as a correspondent bank for Mercantile National Bank, and finally, Mercantile National Bank itself. Initially it appeared that the disturbance had passed.

Depositors who removed funds from banks controlled by Heinze and Morse transferred them to other banks. However, problems involving other banks soon appeared. In October, there was a depositor run on Knickerbocker Trust Company, the third largest trust company in New York City, because of rumors of a connection between Knickerbocker and Morse. Leading New York investment banker J. P. Morgan assembled a group of financiers to consider a private rescue of Knickerbocker. However, they concluded that Knickerbocker was insolvent; therefore, no rescue was attempted. Knickerbocker failed.

The next bank to come under pressure was the Trust Company of America. Morgan's group determined that Trust Company of America was solvent. Morgan declared: "This is the place to stop the trouble, then."[13] Under Morgan's leadership, a group of trust companies and several national banks provided funds to the institution. Secretary of the Treasury George B. Cortelyou agreed to deposit $36 million in New York national banks, specifying that $10 million was to be used for the benefit of ailing trust companies but giving Morgan discretion over the rest.

> The situation was ironic: President Roosevelt had spoken of malefactors of great wealth in terms that implied that Morgan might be included in their number, yet here was his Secretary of the Treasury accepting Morgan's judgment as to how these funds should be disposed. Cortelyou, however, was merely acknowledging, as did Harriman and Rockefeller, that circumstances alter cases. There was a panic raging, it must be stopped. Morgan knew better than anybody else what to do and how to do it, and people did what he told them to.[14]

The crisis soon moved beyond trust companies and commercial banks. A large number of brokerage firms were near failure. The New York Stock Exchange was about to close its doors. Again,

Morgan helped create rescue pools funded by large New York banks. New York City was unable to float a bond issue and was on the edge of bankruptcy. Morgan arranged for his firm and two other banks to purchase the bond issue. Meanwhile, Moore & Schley, one of the nation's largest brokerage firms, teetered on the brink of collapse. Morgan arranged for the brokerage firm to sell its holdings in Tennessee Coal and Iron to U.S. Steel, a move that required President Theodore Roosevelt's approval because of its antitrust implications.

The Panic of 1907 eventually subsided, with one private individual, J. P. Morgan, playing the leading role in responding to the crisis. Secretary of the Treasury Cortelyou provided critical help, staying in constant contact with Morgan and other bankers, as well as providing substantial sums.[15] The panic ushered in a recession, with sharp decreases in commodity prices and industrial production, a large number of bankruptcies, and an increase in unemployment.

One good thing came out of the panic: there was growing public recognition that federal legislation was needed to create a strong mechanism for preventing, or at least addressing, future financial crises. As Senator Nelson W. Aldrich aptly put it, legislation creating a central mechanism was needed because "we may not always have a Pierpont Morgan with us to meet the country's crisis."[16]

The Aldrich Plan

After the panic had subsided, business groups sent numerous petitions to Congress calling for a more elastic currency. Senator Aldrich realized that legislation was necessary to quell public concern. President Theodore Roosevelt mentioned currency elasticity in his annual message to Congress. Warburg launched a campaign for a comprehensive program based on the creation of the "United Reserve Bank," a central bank that would have twenty branches located around the country.

In the postcrisis atmosphere, there was not sufficient time to garner public and political support for comprehensive reform, such as the creation of a central bank. Instead, both houses of Congress passed bills simply providing for greater currency elasticity under the existing fragmented structure. The Senate-House conference committee came up with the Aldrich-Vreeland Act, a stop-gap measure whose provisions were set to expire in 1914. It was passed by both houses of Congress and signed into law by President Roosevelt. The act provided for the issuance of emergency currency backed not only by U.S. government bonds but also other assets on banks' balance sheets, notably commercial paper issued by businesses. Thus, despite its temporary nature, the Aldrich-Vreeland Act ended the long controversy over currency elasticity.[17]

By this point, Glass had served in the House of Representatives without making a major speech. His objections to the Vreeland bill provided the occasion for his first. Glass alleged that it was a measure "for which every Republican Member will vote, but in the provisions of which not one of them honestly believes," comparing this to a description of *Paradise Lost* as "that matchless epic poem which everybody praises and nobody reads." He criticized the bill as creating "an emergency currency," when more was called for: "a careful revision and a wise reformation of the entire banking and currency system of the United States whereby panics may be prevented, or, if not prevented, under which their violence may be diminished and the evils consequent greatly abated."[18] However, Glass did not spell out the type of banking legislation he favored. Moreover, at this point what Glass and his fellow Democrats believed about banking issues counted for little since the Republican majority in the House had increased to 222 Republicans versus 164 Democrats.

In addition to dealing with currency, the Aldrich-Vreeland Act created the National Monetary Commission "to inquire into and report to Congress at the earliest date possible, what changes were necessary or desirable in the monetary system of the United States or in the laws relating to banking and currency." According to financial

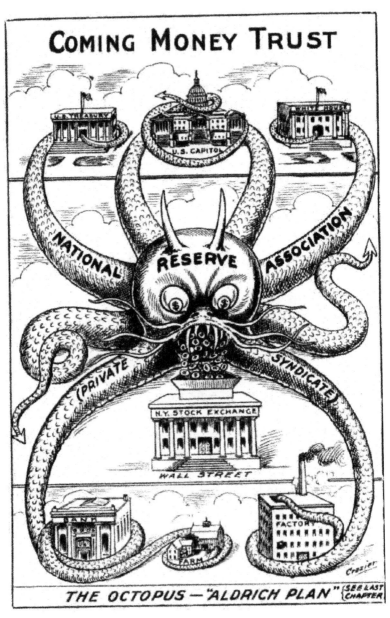

4. The Coming Money Trust. "Octopus – 'Aldrich Plan'," Alfred Owen Crozier, *U.S. Money Vs. Corporation Currency*, 1912.

historian Professor Elmus Wicker, "by removing congressional committee deliberation from its traditional role, Congress believed it would be less partisan and thereby expedite a consensus for permanent banking reform."[19] The commission was made up of nine members of the House and nine senators. Senator Aldrich was the chairman. The commission held extensive public hearings, received numerous monographs from financial experts, visited central banks in several European countries, and issued twenty lengthy reports.

The time looked ripe for action. The Republicans, the party of big business, controlled all three political branches of government—the Senate, the House of Representatives, and the presidency. The key Republican player, Senator Aldrich, now favored creation of a central bank, and he headed the National Monetary Commission.[20] But Aldrich moved slowly. It appears Aldrich believed that Republican control of Congress would be secure forever. In any event, Aldrich was in no rush.[21] The commission did not recommend legislation during the remainder of 1908, or in 1909, 1910, or 1911.

Henry Davison, a partner at J. P. Morgan & Company and a consultant to the commission, suggested to Aldrich that he meet privately with a small group of bankers to draft a banking reform bill. The group met secretly in November 1910 at Jekyll Island, a remote private island off the coast of Georgia that Morgan and other millionaires used as a hunting retreat. Shortly after the meeting, Senator Aldrich unveiled what became known as the "Aldrich Plan," which proposed a reorganization of the American banking system so that it would resemble the European central bank model. It provided for creation of the National Reserve Association located in Washington, DC, with the authority to establish uniform discount rates, buy and sell government securities, and supervise its fifteen branches located in major cities around the country. Each branch would hold the reserves of banks in its area, issue currency notes, discount commercial paper, transfer balances between branches, and perform operating functions such as clearing checks.

The officers of the branches and most of the officers of the National Reserve Association were to be chosen by the participating banks. As Professor Conti-Brown recently emphasized, the association's board "was to have forty-six directors, forty-two of whom—including its three executive officers—were to be appointed directly and indirectly by the banks. The government did not figure into the scene at all."[22] In sum, the Aldrich Plan provided for a centralized reserve banking system controlled by private bankers. It was submitted to Congress in January 1912.

The Aldrich Plan was dead on arrival. In November 1910, the Democrats had won control of the House of Representatives and working control with progressive Republicans of the Senate. The Democrats, who finally had obtained control of Congress, were not about to endorse a conservative Republican financial program. Public concern over the alleged control of the financial system by a small group of private bankers, the so-called "Money Trust," was increasing. In 1911, a major New York City bank, National City Bank, announced that it planned to create a separate company called the National City Co. that would have the same officers and shareholders as the bank, but that could engage in activities that the bank could not engage in directly, such as acquiring interests in other banks or conducting securities activities. The resulting uproar led to the withdrawal of the affiliate plan, but the episode fed public anxiety over the "Money Trust."[23]

The Aldrich Plan was denounced in the Democrats' 1912 platform: "We oppose the so-called Aldrich Bill or the establishment of a central bank, and we believe the people of the country will be largely freed from panics and consequent unemployment and business depressions by such a systematic revision of our banking laws as will render temporary relief in localities where such relief is needed, with protection from control or domination by what is known as the 'money trust.'" The platform of the new Progressive Party headed by ex-president Theodore Roosevelt also rejected the Aldrich Plan, stating, "The issue of currency is fundamentally a government function.... The control should be lodged with the government and should be protected from domination or manipulation by Wall Street or any special interests." Even Republican president Taft threw cold water on the plan by denouncing its core principle of banker control, stating, "but there must be some form of Government supervision and ultimate control, and I favor a reasonable representation of the Government in the management."[24] The Aldrich Plan was not considered by any committee in either house of Congress.

The Republicans had squandered their opportunity for enacting major banking legislation following the Panic of 1907. Senator Aldrich's plan called for a highly centralized system controlled by private banks, a scheme that large banks in the nation's financial centers, along with pro-business Republicans, may have loved, but which most Democrats and Progressives as well as many liberal Republicans found anathema. Perhaps the Aldrich Plan would have been enacted had it been introduced in Congress in 1908, 1909, or 1910. But Aldrich had waited too long. By the time he offered his plan, progressivism was on the ascendancy, and the Democrats had captured both houses of Congress.

The responsibility for banking legislation moved into other hands.

3
AUTHORING THE
FEDERAL RESERVE ACT

At crucial moments, at turning points, when factors appear more or less equally balanced, chance, individuals and their decisions and acts, themselves not necessarily predictable—indeed, seldom so— can determine the course of history.

—Sir Isaiah Berlin

In February 1912, the chairman of the House Banking Committee named Glass to chair a subcommittee charged with developing reserve banking legislation. Glass drafted a proposal for a decentralized system of regional reserve banks under the supervision of the Comptroller of the Currency. President-elect Wilson supported the proposal, with the substitution for the Comptroller of a Federal Reserve Board consisting exclusively of public members. Glass's bill was opposed by Republicans, who supported the Aldrich Plan, and by agrarian Democrats, who viewed Glass's bill as a disguised version of the Aldrich Plan. Glass led the successful drive to enact the Federal Reserve Act.

Creation of Two House Subcommittees

While Senator Aldrich and big city bankers reacted to the Panic of 1907 by seeking the enactment of reserve banking legislation, others responded in quite a different way. Some radical Democrats and progressive Republicans alleged that J. P. Morgan and his Wall Street allies had caused the panic in order to enrich themselves. Republican Representative Charles A. Lindbergh of Minnesota expressed concern over the so-called "Money Trust." On December 4, 1911, Lindbergh introduced a resolution calling upon Congress to appoint a committee to look into the matter. Later that same month, Samuel Untermyer, a well-known New York attorney, intensified concern with an address before the Financial Forum in New York entitled "Is There a Money Trust." Untermyer answered his question in the affirmative: "If ... we mean by this loose elastic term 'Trust'... that there is a close and well defined 'community of interest' and understanding among the men who dominate the financial destinies of our country ... our investigators will find a situation confronting us far more serious than is popularly supposed to exist."[1]

The press took up the cry. The *New York Times* described bankers as "the trust of trusts, without whose favor all other trusts must languish a lingering death." The *Washington Post* called upon Congress "to settle once and for all the question whether a small group of men control the financial and business destiny of the nation."[2]

The House of Representatives, now controlled by Democrats, authorized the Banking and Currency Committee, chaired by Congressman Arsène P. Pujo of Louisiana, to conduct an investigation. Pujo divided his committee into two subcommittees. One subcommittee, chaired by Pujo, was to investigate the alleged Money Trust. The second subcommittee, chaired by Glass, was to develop reserve banking legislation.[3]

The Pujo Subcommittee

Pujo appointed Untermyer counsel to his subcommittee. Pujo was a mere figurehead of his subcommittee; Untermyer ran the show and did a brilliant job: "Mr. Untermyer swiftly demonstrated his immense knowledge of high finance and his extraordinary ability and merciless diligence as an examiner.... And the admissions that he obtained from their [bankers'] reluctant and haughty lips justified most of the accusations about a Money Trust that he had been making." Untermyer was equally successful in obtaining press coverage: "He issued stupendous statements from his New York office.... Lengthy as they were, however, these handouts were usually hot enough to land on the front pages."[4]

In February 1913, the Pujo subcommittee issued a detailed report. While the report admitted that that the hearings had not demonstrated the existence of a Money Trust in strictly legal terms, it asserted that "surprisingly many of the elements of such a combination exist," and concluded that "the situation is fraught with too great peril to our institutions to be tolerated."[5]

The subcommittee's report then set forth recommendations for legislation.[6] In the area of commercial banks, the report proposed that the same person be prohibited from serving as a director of more than one bank located in the same geographic area; that national banks be prohibited from underwriting and dealing in securities; and that national banks be prohibited from being affiliated with securities companies.[7] In the area of securities activities, the report recommended that securities firms be prohibited from taking corporate deposits; that corporations whose securities are listed on a stock exchange be required to file information with the exchange that would be open to public inspection; and that purchasers of securities be required to put up at least 20 percent of the purchase price (20 percent "margin"). These securities provisions were to be administered by the Post Office Department because the Constitution gave Congress authority over the mails.

The Pujo subcommittee's recommendations were not taken up by Congress since President Wilson did not want to get into a fight with Wall Street. However, as discussed in subsequent chapters, the New Deal's reform program of 1933–34 included many of the subcommittee's recommendations.

In the short-term, the Pujo subcommittee's hearings riveted public attention on the financial sector and the dangers it posed to American society. For eight months, the subcommittee, led by its counsel, Samuel Untermyer, "frightened the nation" with its revelations.[8] Public concern increased when another crusading attorney, Louis D. Brandeis, authored a series of articles based on the Pujo hearings (later published as the book *Other People's Money and How the Bankers Use It*). Brandeis sent the articles in draft form to President-elect Woodrow Wilson, who read them carefully, making notes in the margins. They confirmed Wilson's belief in the Money Trust and convinced him that some form of public supervision of the banking system was needed.[9] Thus, while the Pujo subcommittee did not make recommendations regarding reserve banking legislation because jurisdiction of that area was lodged in Glass's subcommittee, its dramatic hearings greatly increased the chances for enactment of that legislation. The exact nature of that reserve banking legislation remained to be decided.[10]

Development of a Reserve Banking Bill

Glass and his subcommittee faced a formidable task in developing reserve banking legislation. First, Glass had to decide what type of reserve banking system he personally wanted, in terms of both structure and the role of government. He opposed the Aldrich Plan because he believed "it was so arranged that the larger banks of the country must inevitably become predominant," and that money would flow from smaller banks across the country to big city banks to fund "stock speculative operations at the money centers." Instead, Glass favored a decentralized system using a number of regional banks, who "could better be expected to minister to the immediate financial and commercial requirements of their respective territories."[11] As to the role of government, we have seen that Glass's racism and views of Reconstruction made him hostile to an activist federal government. He therefore wanted to keep federal government influence over any reserve banking system to a minimum.

Second, it would be extremely difficult to devise a system that could garner sufficient political support to have a chance of enactment. Opinions differed widely as to what form reserve banking legislation should take. Big city bankers wanted a single central bank that would be supervised by private bankers, the scheme set forth in the Aldrich Plan. Bankers and businessmen in the South and West, like Glass, feared both Wall Street and federal government dominance and therefore wanted a system of private regional banks. Southern and western agrarians also favored a regional system, but wanted it to be controlled by government, not private bankers. Republican insurgents and Progressives favored a single central bank that was controlled by the federal government. As John Milton Cooper has observed, "In short, two conflicting principles—private versus public control and decentralization versus centralization—created a veritable Gordian knot that a successful program of banking reform would have to cut."[12]

Third, banking issues were highly partisan. The Democrats had opposed and helped block enactment of the Aldrich Plan. Republicans could be expected to retaliate against any scheme put forth by Democrats.

Finally, as the experiences with Presidents Theodore Roosevelt and Taft demonstrated, banking legislation was unlikely to be enacted without strong presidential leadership. When Glass assumed the chairmanship of his subcommittee in April 1912, he had no idea who the next president would be, nor whether the new chief executive might have any interest in fostering reserve banking legislation.

In the face of these obstacles, Glass began his work. Fortunately, Glass had been diligently studying banking issues since his appointment to the House Banking and Currency Committee in 1903. Glass realized that he and the other members of his subcommittee lacked the training and background needed to formulate highly technical banking and currency legislation. Therefore, Glass's first step as subcommittee chairman was to appoint, as expert adviser to the subcommittee, Dr. Henry Parker Willis. Willis had taught Glass's two sons at Washington and Lee University and had been the Washington, DC, correspondent for the *Journal of Commerce*. Glass selected Willis precisely because he was "convinced that Dr. Willis entertained views akin to his own definite idea of establishing a system of regional banks."[13]

Glass and Willis began their work by adopting a series of general and tentative principles to guide the drafting of reserve banking legislation. Among these principles were:

> Whatever is done should seek to provide a permanent basis of banking organization, regularly functioning and regularly incorporated or established. ¶The basis of organization may well be modeled upon the experience of American bankers in their clearing house organizations, in so far as the latter have to do with joint action for effecting interbank payments. ¶Data, expedients, mechanisms, and modes of procedure found in the various plans already before the Committee may be considered, and where needful modified and used. Indeed, if a desirable feature be found in any of the plans, that is a fact which should commend it rather than militate against it. ¶In general, the new bill should seek to provide for cooperative action on the part of the banks and should accept the principle of centralization under suitable government oversight and control.[14]

By the end of October 1912, Willis had drafted a bill based on these principles. It provided for a decentralized, privately controlled reserve banking system, with twenty or more independent reserve banks located in major cities around the nation. Like the Aldrich Plan, it provided for private control. However, it rejected the Aldrich Plan's centralization and potential Wall Street control in favor of a regional approach.

The November elections produced a Democratic landslide. Because of the three-way contest among Republican President William Howard Taft, Progressive candidate Theodore Roosevelt, and Democrat Woodrow Wilson, Wilson was elected president. The Democrats increased their control of the House of Representatives to a huge margin of 290 to 127. The Democrats even gained control of the Senate, with a plurality of 51 to 44. The Democrats now controlled the White House, the House of Representatives, and the Senate. Reform, including banking and currency reform, was in the air, and the Democrats were in a position to capitalize on the mood.

Glass thought that elements of both parties would support banking and currency legislation provided it was backed by a forceful and determined president. Therefore, Glass wrote to President-elect Wilson to congratulate him on his victory, fill him in on the subcommittee's work, and request a meeting in order to obtain "some suggestions from you as to the nature of the work already done and as to what you think should be done."[15] Wilson replied that he would contact Glass after a short vacation in Bermuda "because the question of the revision of the currency is one of such capital importance that I wish to devote the most serious and immediate attention to it."[16]

As Glass was preparing for his meeting with the president-elect, the first crisis hit. Untermyer informed Willis that he intended to have the *Pujo subcommittee* introduce reserve banking legislation, the one area that had been delegated to Glass's subcommittee. Even worse from Glass's point of view, the legislation would be based on the Aldrich Plan. In addition, Pujo was about to retire from the House of Representatives, and Glass saw Untermyer's move as an attempt to prevent him from succeeding to the chairmanship of the full House Banking and Currency Committee. Glass immediately complained to Pujo, who telegraphed Glass on November 11th that his subcommittee had no intention of taking up a currency bill: "Information that sub-committee of which I am chairman contemplates or ever has contemplated the assertion of right to deal with the Aldrich currency bill now being considered by sub-committee of which you are chairman is absolutely without foundation in fact. On the contrary, I have refused to consider such proposed action." Apparently, Untermyer still continued to seek involvement in reserve banking legislation. On December 3, Glass wrote to Willis that his subcommittee had rejected Untermyer's attempt to "coalesce" the two subcommittees.[7]

Glass had squelched Untermyer's attempts to seize jurisdiction of the reserve banking issue. The incident marked the beginning of a long and bitter rivalry between the two men. Glass came to despise Untermyer, later stating, "I ... plainly told him in writing that I regarded him as an incorrigible scamp. President Wilson wouldn't let him come to the White House. He made his money years ago by practicing the very illicit swindling transactions that he now affects to disapprove." Glass later claimed that he had attempted, unsuccessfully, to prevent Untermyer from being named as counsel to the Pujo subcommittee.[18]

On December 26, 1912, Glass and Willis traveled to Princeton, New Jersey, to meet with President-elect Wilson. They outlined their plan for a system of regional reserve banks. National banks would be required to subscribe to the stock of the regional reserve banks and to deposit their reserve funds with them. State-chartered banks would be permitted to participate on a voluntary basis. National bank notes backed by government bonds would be replaced with notes backed by both gold and liquid commercial paper. The system would be supervised by the Comptroller of the Currency, an official in the Department of the Treasury in Washington, DC, who oversaw national banks.

Glass emphasized to Wilson the importance of a decentralized system and the need to prevent Wall Street control. Wilson agreed to the entire plan with one exception—placing supervision of the system in the Comptroller of the Currency. The president-elect declared that the comptroller was "already tsaristic head of the national banking system of the country." He stated that instead of using the comptroller, there should be a "a capstone" placed upon the regional structure in the form of a new "altruistic Federal Reserve Board at Washington to supervise the proposed system." While Glass personally was troubled that such a board smacked too much of centralization, he told Willis to incorporate the idea into the draft bill, stating: "I would cheerfully go with the president-elect for some body of central supervisory control, if such a body can be constituted and divested of the practical attributes of a central bank," and "I think we should have the central mechanism in readiness if we must yield to this idea."[19]

The meeting with President-elect Wilson was a huge success for Glass. With one change (regarding the specific supervisor of the system), Wilson had accepted Glass's entire plan for a decentralized reserve banking system and had agreed to put the full weight of his presidency behind it. Wilson later admitted that he, like President Theodore Roosevelt before him, was terribly confused by banking issues: "It is not like the tariff, about which opinion has been definitely forming long years through. There are almost as many judgments as there are men. To form a single plan and a single intention about it seems at times a task so various and so elusive that it is hard to keep one's heart from failing."[20] However, whereas Roosevelt's confusion led him to decline to get into the battle over banking reform, Wilson committed himself to joining the battle, and on Glass's side.

Three days after the Wilson-Glass-Willis meeting, Glass sent Wilson a letter warning that they could expect strong opposition from the commercial banking sector and outlining his proposed legislative strategy. He planned to offer legislation providing for a decentralized regional reserve banking system, leaving it to supporters of the Aldrich Plan to propose the addition of a top "superstructure," which would demonstrate the dangers of bank monopoly and centralized power:

> Might it not be well to draft a bill on the Regional Reserve Bank lines, taking care of all the details discussed last Thursday and put on the advocates of the Aldrich bill the burden of showing that a central superstructure should be imposed, requiring them to suggest a superstructure that that shall not possess the evils of bank monopoly and the dangers of centralized power? We may ourselves have in readiness such a "capstone" as I understood you to suggest having the wholesome powers of a central supervisory control.[21]

However, Glass decided not take this approach, likely because of Wilson's desires. He amended his bill, as Wilson had proposed, to provide for a "capstone" in the form of a Federal Reserve Board.

Now that he had the backing of the president-elect, Glass worked to obtain the support of big city bankers who previously had supported the Aldrich Plan. He met with bankers privately and arranged for a round of hearings with the bankers as witnesses.

> The hearings of Glass's subcommittee in January and February 1913 were nothing less than a love feast. A. Barton Hepburn [of the Chase National Bank] started by assuring the Congressmen that the American Bankers Association would cooperate "on any good measure" that led to elasticity and cooperation in money reserve management.... He was followed by Warburg, who assured the subcommittee that the Aldrich Plan was one way, but not the only one, to solve the banking problem.... ¶Festus J. Wade, St. Louis banker and member of the currency committee of the ABA, indicated that "this association will cooperate with any and all people

5. "The Man Who Was Pushed Into Politics," *Chicago Daily News*, 1913.

in devising a financial system for this country," even though he personally favored the Aldrich Bill. "Any bill you submit will be a vast improvement on our present system," and even if were called "central supervisory control" rather than a "central bank."[22]

Thereafter, Glass requested a second meeting with President-elect Wilson. On January 30, 1913, Glass and Willis traveled to Trenton, New Jersey. Glass reported to Wilson on the successful hearings and his personal meetings with big city bankers. He gave Wilson a new draft of his bill, which provided for a system of fifteen or more regional reserve banks that would perform central banking functions. Overseeing the system would be a Federal Reserve Board composed of six public members and three bankers chosen indirectly by directors of the regional banks. Wilson's response was "Go ahead!" Moreover, Wilson assured Glass that he would oppose any effort to block Glass's succession to the chairmanship of the House Banking and Currency Committee.[23]

Glass was succeeding. The president-elect was behind his bill. Big city bankers, who previously had backed the Aldrich Plan, seemed to be coming around to supporting Glass's bill. Glass had blocked Untermyer's attempt to take jurisdiction over reserve banking legislation away from Glass's subcommittee. Glass was headed toward becoming chairman of the House Banking and Currency Committee, a key position in any effort to enact banking and currency legislation. Things soon got even better. In May, the House passed the first major tariff reduction since 1857, a huge victory for the Wilson Administration. Wilson targeted banking and currency legislation as his administration's next major legislative priority.

Then a problem hit. It did not come from a likely source such as Wall Street bankers, conservative businessmen, or stalwart supporters of the Aldrich Plan. It came from the very heart of the Wilson Administration, Secretary of State William Jennings Bryan.

Glass had been concerned about Bryan, who had long called for government control of the banking system and for exclusive government-issuance, rather than bank-issuance, of currency. Glass urged the president to try to preempt any possible problem by meeting with Bryan.[24] The president invited Bryan to the White House and pleaded with him to support Glass's bill. Bryan refused, insisting that the Federal Reserve Board should consist exclusively of public members and that only the federal government should have the authority to issue the nation's currency.

The difficulties soon intensified. On May 21, 1913, Willis met with Senator Robert L. Owen, chairman of the Senate Banking Committee and a Bryan Democrat. Owen was clearly resentful of the discussions that had taken place among Wilson, Glass, and Willis both before and after Wilson's inauguration. He raised the same objections Bryan had about private banker representation on the Federal Reserve Board and bank issuance of currency.

Secretary of the Treasury McAdoo sought to devise a solution to the controversy. He met with Bryan, Owen, Untermyer, and several bankers to outline a new bill. It called for the establishment of a central bank, the National Reserve, located in the Treasury Department. The National Reserve would have fifteen branches. The system would be administered by a National Reserve Board consisting entirely of public members. Currency could only be issued by a National Currency Commission, also located in the Treasury Department. The proposal was designed to appeal to big city bankers by providing for a highly centralized reserve banking system and to Bryanites by providing for exclusive public control of the system and exclusive government issuance of currency.

Glass was stunned by McAdoo's proposal and feared that Wilson might be tempted to back McAdoo's plan in order to gain Bryan's and Owen's support. Glass fought back with everything he had. He contacted A. Barton Hepburn of the Chase National Bank, urging him to rally his bank friends to oppose the McAdoo Plan since it was "an utter perversion of the true function of government" and was "unique and untried." Hepburn complied. Glass contacted Owen. Willis contacted McAdoo. Glass met with President Wilson and pleaded with him to disavow McAdoo's plan. Wilson agreed, saying, "I fear Mac is deceived" and "but fortunately the thing has not gone so far it cannot be stopped."[25] As a consequence, McAdoo agreed to withdraw his plan and support Glass's bill.[26]

While the McAdoo plan had been taken off the table, the fundamental split between Glass, on the one hand, and Bryan and Owen, on the other, remained. Given the importance of the issues and the high government officials involved, only the president could resolve the matter. Wilson's biographer, Arthur S. Link, has concluded that since 1910, Wilson had been developing two basic assumptions with respect to banking legislation. The first was that the concentration of credit and money in Wall Street had reached the proportions of a monopoly. Wilson supported the regional reserve bank concept as a means of countering the alleged "Money Trust." Wilson's second assumption was that banking was so much of a public business that government must share in making fundamental financial decisions, although the details were of less importance.[27]

Wilson decided that he would not make a decision on the Glass versus Bryan-Owen split until he consulted with his chief economic adviser, Louis D. Brandeis. He did so on June 11, 1913. Brandeis came down firmly on Bryan's and Owen's side as to the government's supreme position.

Regarding the members of the Federal Reserve Board, Brandeis stated, "The American people will not be content to have the discretion necessarily involved vested in a Board composed wholly or in part of bankers; for their judgment may be biased by private interests or affiliation." As to the issuance of currency, he said, "The power to issue currency should be vested exclusively in Government officials, even when the currency is issued against commercial paper."[28]

Meanwhile, Glass continued to believe that it was essential to have three private bankers on the Federal Reserve Board. On June 18, Glass wrote to the president, "The matter has given me much concern, and more than ever I am convinced that it will be a grave mistake to alter so radically the feature of the bill."[29] However, that very day the president summoned Glass, Owen, and McAdoo to the White House and told them that there had to be *exclusive* government control of the Federal Reserve Board and that Federal Reserve notes had to be obligations of the U.S. government. Glass quietly accepted Wilson's decisions in favor of Bryan and Owen, a deft political move that was to pay huge dividends as he worked for passage of legislation.

The Wilson Administration's Drive for Legislation

Now that all members of the Wilson Administration and Democratic congressional leaders were united, they could go on the offensive. Glass provided the text of his revised bill to the press. Wilson arranged a White House meeting with all of the Democratic members of the House Banking and Currency Committee. Secretary of State Bryan announced that he would use his influence in Congress to obtain enactment of the bill.

On June 23, 1913, Wilson addressed a joint session of Congress to call for enactment of the Federal Reserve bill. Wilson hit all of the notes—the need for currency elasticity, mobilization of reserves, decentralization, avoiding use of bank reserves for speculation, and government oversight:

> We must have a currency, not rigid as now, but readily, elastically responsive to sound credit, the expanding and contracting credits of everyday transactions, the normal ebb and flow of personal and corporate dealings. Our banking laws must mobilize reserves; must not permit the concentration anywhere in a few hands of the monetary resources of the country or their use for speculative

purposes in such volume as to hinder or impede or stand in the way of other more legitimate, more fruitful uses. And the control of the system of banking and of issue which our new laws are to set up must be public, not private, must be vested in the Government itself, so that the banks may be the instruments, not the masters, of business and of individual enterprise and initiative.... I have come to you, as the head of the Government and the responsible leader of the party in power, to urge action, now while there is time to serve the country deliberately and as we should, in a clear air of common counsel."[30]

The response of the traditional conservative banking and business communities to the Glass-Owen bill was swift and angry. McAdoo wrote that "there was a general belief on the part of bankers that governmental control of the Federal Reserve System would be ruinous."[31]

The *Banking Law Journal* called the bill "a proposal for the creation of a vast engine of political domination over the great forces of profitable American industry and internal commerce," and announced that "the fight is now for the protection of private rights." A *New York Times* editorial declared that "the measure goes to the very extreme in establishing absolute political control over the business of banking." A banker from San Antonio wrote, "it is a communistic idea that is sought to be written into the financial statutes of the country."[32]

Wilson's biographer, Arthur S. Link, has observed that these vehement attacks stemmed from conservatives' fear that the bill represented a major break from America's traditional adherence to *laissez faire* in the field of banking and the start of government intervention in the very heart of the capitalistic system.[33]

McAdoo viewed the opposition in more political terms:

At the core of its [the business world's] critical objection was a profound opposition to the Democratic Administration. Almost all of the leading financiers and bankers—and representatives, generally, of Wall Street interests—were Republicans. Like those ancient shriveled sages, mentioned in the Bible, who knew that no good could come out of Nazareth, they were convinced that something or other must be wrong with anything conceived by the Democratic Party. They thought, without a shadow of excuse for thinking so, that the Administration had set out consciously to cripple the banking business.[34]

The administration sought to bring around leading bankers to support, or at least not oppose, the bill. On June 24, 1913, the president, Glass, McAdoo, and Owen met with a group of big city bankers. The administration agreed to changes in the bill, but when the bankers pressed for their most important wish, private banker representation on the Federal Reserve Board, Wilson turned them down flat, asking two rhetorical questions: "Will one of you gentlemen tell me in what civilized country of the earth there are important government boards of control on which private interests are represented?" and "Which of you gentlemen thinks that the railroads should select members of the Interstate Commerce Commission?"[35] Wilson later agreed to a change in the bill that provided for a Federal Advisory Council, consisting of representatives of regional banks. It was designed to act as a liaison between regional banks and the governmental board. However, this and other changes were not sufficient to bring bankers on board. Wilson, Glass, McAdoo, Owen, and Bryan geared up for battle with the banking and business establishment.

Then a major assault came from an unexpected quarter—southern and western agrarian Democratic members of the House of Representatives. These men had been long-time supporters of Bryan.

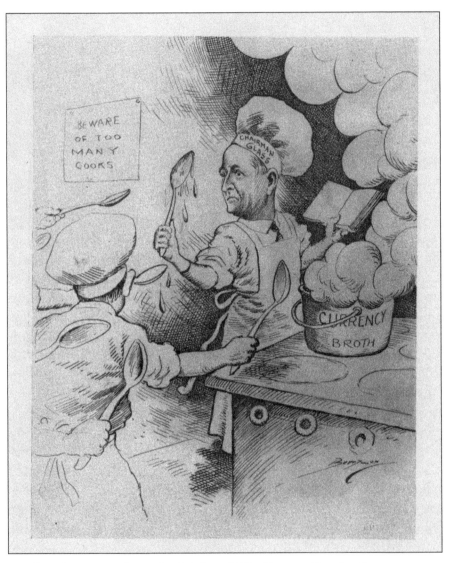

6. "The Chairman Clears the Kitchen," Washington *Evening Star*, 1913.

They hated Wall Street. The recent Pujo hearings on the Money Trust had increased their already high level of concern. Willis wrote that these men were convinced that "the Federal Reserve Act was essentially a disguised form of the Aldrich Bill, and that it would play into the hands of the money power by enabling the bankers of the city to obtain the use of funds belonging to country bankers which the latter ought for the welfare of the people to keep at home and to employ in local loans."[36]

The agrarians attacked the Federal Reserve bill. On July 12, 1913, Representative Robert L. Henry of Texas, chairman of the powerful House Rules Committee, introduced a resolution calling for a resumption of the Money Trust investigation. This was a direct challenge to Wilson's leadership of the Democratic Party and to Glass's authority as the new chairman of the House Banking Committee.[37] Agrarian Democrats on the House Banking and Currency Committee introduced a series of amendments to the Federal Reserve bill. On July 23, 1913, a majority of the committee, over Glass's objection, adopted an amendment sponsored by Representative Otis T. Wingo of Arkansas prohibiting interlocking bank directorships. The next day, Representative J. Willard Ragsdale of South Carolina offered a series of amendments, including one providing for the issuance of currency based on warehouse receipts for cotton, corn, and wheat. On July 31, 1913, Representative Joe E. Eagle of Texas issued a statement damning the Glass bill as a mere disguise of the Aldrich Plan.

President Wilson and Glass worked hard to beat back the agrarian radicals, conceding a few of their points, but opposing most. The savior was the long-time leader of the agrarian wing of the Democratic Party, Secretary of State William Jennings Bryan. Bryan sent Glass a letter that Glass read to the House Democratic caucus:

> You are authorized to speak for me and say that I appreciate so profoundly the services rendered by the President to the people in the stand that he has taken on

the fundamental principles involved, that I am with him in all the details. If my opinion has influence with anyone who is called upon to act on this measure, I am willing to assume full responsibility for what I do when I advise him to stand by the President and assist in securing the passage of this measure at the earliest possible moment.[38]

Wilson's kid-gloves treatment of Bryan and Glass's decision to quietly accede to Bryan on key issues had paid off significantly.

Bryan's intervention broke the opposition. The Democratic caucus voted 116 to 9 to approve the Federal Reserve bill. The bill was approved by the House Committee on Banking and Currency. On September 18, 1913, the House of Representatives passed the bill by a vote of 285 to 85. All but three Democrats voted for the bill, as did twenty-three Republicans and ten Progressives.

House passage of the Federal Reserve bill was a major triumph for the Wilson Administration. Many people, including Wilson, Bryan, and McAdoo played critical roles. However, Glass was the key actor. McAdoo wrote him:

You are, more than any other single man, entitled to the credit for this real victory in the cause of the people of this country, and your name will always be linked with the first constructive financial measure passed by Congress since the enactment of the National Banking Act. You have led the fight with singular ability and with a high order of statesmanship.[39]

Glass realized that Bryan had saved the day in the House of Representatives and was likely to be an important player when the bill was taken up by the Senate. Therefore, Glass wrote to Bryan:

We are immensely indebted to you for effective aid in critical periods of the contest in committee and in caucus.... you have disappointed your enemies and pleased your friends by standing firmly with the President for sound legislation in behalf of the American people. The country and your party are greatly obliged to you for the skill and discernment with which you have helped along the fight, and I am particularly grateful.[40]

Initially, the Senate looked like quite a good forum for the administration's drive for reserve banking legislation. However, as McAdoo observed, "The Glass-Owen Bill was beset by perils in its passage through the Senate; time and time again it was on the verge of shipwreck."[41] This was because the administration was weakest where it counted most—in the Senate Committee on Banking and Currency, the body that had to report a reserve banking bill to the full Senate.

There were seven Democrats and five Republicans on the committee. In addition to Chairman Owen, three other Democrats were favorably inclined toward the bill. But three Democrats—Gilbert M. Hitchcock of Nebraska, James O'Gorman of New York, and James A. Reed of Missouri—were hostile to the bill for reasons having nothing to do with its merits. Each had personal grievances with President Wilson relating to issues involving patronage and Wilson's general attitude toward Congress. These three unhappy Democrats might ally themselves with the five Republicans on the committee and prevent progress on the legislation.

This is precisely what initially occurred. The coalition of three disgruntled Democrats and five Republicans forced Chairman Owen to hold hearings on banking and currency legislation that stretched from September 2 to October 27, 1913. The bank witnesses at the hearings and bankers elsewhere used the occasion to attack the Federal Reserve bill.

Although the bill had passed Glass's own body, the House, Glass assisted the push for legislation in the Senate. In early October, Glass gave a speech warning bankers that delay was not their friend:

> The time for action on this great question is now, while the public interest is alive, and while we can act with that caution and deliberation which is impossible when the country is in the throes of a financial panic. To those who advocate further delay in the hope thereby of securing legislation which they consider more conservative or more favorable to the banking interests, I say with all the seriousness at my command, that they are pursuing a false hope. The most vigorous opposition to this bill has been from those who want a more radical measure. If legislation now is postponed until the public is goaded by another panic, you may rest assured that the resulting legislation will be more, far more radical—yes, far more radical than that contained in the present bill.[42]

President Wilson fumed. He threatened to campaign around the country for the bill, particularly visiting the home states of the three Democratic opponents. He demanded, unsuccessfully, that the Senate Democratic caucus discipline the three men. But finally, Wilson and Glass realized that they would have to compromise with the rebels. On October 16, 1913, Wilson invited the three Democratic senators to the White House and invited their suggestions for changes in the Federal Reserve bill. Wilson thought that his efforts were making progress.

But on October 23, 1913, Frank A. Vanderlip, president of the National City Bank, testified before the Senate Banking Committee and delivered a bombshell. Vanderlip presented a new banking and currency plan that he had prepared at the request of the three Democratic insurgents and one Republican senator. The Vanderlip plan provided for a single strong central bank, the Federal Reserve Bank of

7. President Wilson signing the Federal Reserve Act; painting by Wilbur
G. Kurtz (Glass is third from right). Courtesy of the Woodrow Wilson
Presidential Library, Staunton, Virginia.

the United States, which would have twelve branches located around
the country. The federal government would have exclusive control
of the system. The Vanderlip plan essentially was a revised version
of the highly centralized Aldrich Plan, but with government, rather
than private, control. McAdoo later wrote, "It was decidedly amusing
to read the favorable comments of some of these same bankers on
the Vanderlip plan, which contained provisions to which they had
expressed themselves as unalterably opposed, but which, dressed up
in a National City Bank costume, took on an alluring mien."[43]

Wilson and Glass smelled a rat, believing that the Vanderlip plan
was designed to stop the forward motion of the Federal Reserve

bill and prevent the enactment of *any* legislation. When Vanderlip requested an opportunity to meet with the president in person,
Wilson turned him down:

> I am at a loss to understand how you can have come
> to think of the bank plan which you have proposed as
> "being along the lines of my own thought." It is so far
> as being along the lines of my thought in this matter
> that it would be quite useless for me to discuss it with
> you.... I thought I had made it clear to the whole country
> that I was earnestly and unqualifiedly in favor of all the
> main features of the bill recently passed by the House of
> Representatives and now in the Senate.[44]

The Senate Committee on Banking and Currency proceeded to report
two bills to the Senate—a slightly amended version of the administration's Federal Reserve bill and a bill embodying the Vanderlip
plan. Meanwhile, the public was getting increasingly fed up with the
Senate's delay. There was growing business and bank support for the
Federal Reserve bill that had been passed by the House. Finally, on
December 19, 1913, the Senate voted down a modified version of the
Vanderlip plan in a close vote of 44 to 41. The Senate then approved
the Federal Reserve bill by a vote of 54 to 34. Every Democrat, including the three insurgents, voted in favor, as did five Republicans and
one Progressive.

The House and Senate bills then went to a conference committee,
which reconciled differences. On December 22, 1913, the final bill was
approved by the House, 298 to 60, and by the Senate, 43 to 25. That
same evening, President Wilson signed the Federal Reserve Act into
law. As Professor Link has commented, "thus ended the long struggle
for the greatest single piece of legislation of the Wilson era and one
of the most important domestic Acts in the nation's history."[45]

Paul M. Warburg, who had opposed many of Glass's positions but

who worked for passage of the final bill, wrote to Glass, "You are entitled to the thanks of the Nation for the hard, conscientious and able
work that you have done."[46] On December 25, 1913, President Wilson
wrote to Glass, "May I express my admiration for the way in which
you have carried the fight for the currency bill to an extraordinarily
successful issue. I hope and believe that the whole country appre-
ciates the work you have done at something like its real value and I
rejoice that you have so established yourself in its confidence."[47]

The Post-Game Debate(s)

Enactment of the Federal Reserve Act in December 1913 had been
an extraordinary accomplishment. The *Elmira Star-Gazette* wrote
on February 27, 1914, "to arrange the details, to work out a plan that
would be satisfactory to all, to business men and to bankers alike,
to the big banks and the small banks, such as this bill has proved
to be, was a task for an Hercules." Subsequent writers evinced the
same admiration for the act. In 1935, Frederick Lewis Allen called the
act a "masterly compromise" since it "provided indeed for a super-
banking system, but a decentralized one (to meet the jealousy and
suspicion of the small cities) which while operated by men chosen
by the private bankers (to placate the banking community) would be
supervised and regulated by a government board (to prevent Wall
Street control)."[48]

Given the recognized importance of the act and the strong per-
sonalities who had been involved in its development and enactment,
it is not surprising that many of these individuals claimed credit
for the act. As could have been predicted, Untermyer asserted that
the act was "the direct outcome of the disclosures of the dangerous
concentration of the control of money and credits by the Pujo inves-
tigating Committee," the subcommittee that Untermyer had run.
Senator Owen published a book stressing his contribution. Warburg
emphasized the importance of the Aldrich Plan that he had helped

develop. Glass and Willis took the other side, explicitly emphasizing the role played by President Wilson (and implicitly emphasizing the roles they had played), belittling the importance of the Aldrich Plan. Yale Professor Charles Seymour wrote a book emphasizing the role of a player who had not been very visible during the battle, President Wilson's adviser Colonel Edward M. House.[49] The post-game debate over who should get credit for the Federal Reserve Act illustrates President Kennedy's observation, "victory has a hundred fathers."

In fact, there are two separate debates, which often get confused with one another. First, who deserves credit for the provisions of the Federal Reserve Act? Second, who deserves credit for steering the act through Congress?

Authorship of the Act's Provisions

Shortly after enactment of the act, a furious debate broke out regarding the degree to which the act was based on the Aldrich Plan. Three key players—Carter Glass, H. Parker Willis, and Nelson Aldrich—all maintained that the Aldrich Plan did *not* form the basis for the Federal Reserve Act.

Glass asserted, "It passes all comprehension, in view of this authentic record, how any person can expect to be believed when he asserts that the Federal Reserve Act is, in either a practical or theoretical sense, an imitation of the Aldrich currency scheme." Willis declared "the Federal Reserve Act ... had little or no relationship in principle to the so-called Aldrich bill." Aldrich gave an address criticizing the Federal Reserve Act, and Glass acutely observed that it was doubtful that Aldrich "would have been foolish enough to excoriate bitterly ... a piece of legislation which had been patterned after his own production."[50]

However, Warburg undertook a detailed line-by-line, provision-by-provision comparison of the Aldrich Plan and the act, and stated, "for our part we believe that the evidence adduced from these comparisons will warrant the conclusion that there is a very distinct relationship between the two bills and that, instead of differing in 'principle, purpose, and processes,' they are surprisingly akin." In 2005, Professor Elmus Wicker undertook a similar comparison and reached the same conclusion.[51] During Glass's lifetime, most historians came to agree with Warburg. Frederick Lewis Allen stated that the Wilson Administration "took over the Aldrich-Warburg idea and altered it to make it a part of the reform program." Alexander Dana Noyes wrote that Wilson introduced his plan aggressively "embodying in it much of the Aldrich Plan's proposed machinery."[52]

However, this is only part of the story. While many "technical" provisions of the act came from the Aldrich Plan, the act's "political" provisions, those dealing with decentralization and governance, were new.

When Senator Aldrich and his advisers sat down to devise a reserve banking system, they followed the existing schemes in England, France, and Germany. There would be a single powerful reserve bank. As Professor Conti-Brown recently emphasized, Aldrich's creation was aptly entitled the *National* Reserve Association.[53] This approach flew in the face of traditional American hostility to centralized financial control dating back to the Jacksonian era. In contrast, in 1912 when Glass began work on his bill, he immediately decided to work for a highly decentralized system. Glass stated that his Federal Reserve System was "modelled upon our federal political system. It establishes a group of independent but affiliated and sympathetic sovereignties, working on their own responsibility in local affairs, but united in national affairs by a superior body which is conducted from the national point of view. The regional banks are the states and the Federal Reserve Board is the Congress."[54] Glass's creation was aptly entitled the *Federal* Reserve System.

Aldrich's biographer, Nathaniel Wright Stephenson, wrote bitterly about the difference between Aldrich's "scientific" approach and Glass's less sophisticated "political" approach.[55] This criticism misses the point. Aldrich's tin ear to public opposition to centralization likely doomed his bill to failure even if he had not delayed its introduction in Congress. Glass's understanding of this political reality and his use of a decentralized federal approach gave his bill a fighting chance. Ironically, it was Thomas W. Lamont, a partner of J. P. Morgan & Co. and a biographer of one of the key New York bankers who worked with Aldrich, Henry P. Davison, who best described Glass's political acumen in adopting a decentralized federal approach, "The scheme of regional central institutions, each with note-issuing privilege, but subject to supervision by the Federal Reserve Board at Washington, served to please the local pride of these various regions and to gain readier support in Congress. This was a perfectly legitimate consideration for Representative Carter Glass (as he then was) and his associates, handling the legislation at Washington, to have in mind."[56]

President Wilson added a second "political" element to the act by insisting that there be exclusive public control of the reserve banking system. Glass's revised bill provided that the Federal Reserve Board would have six public members and three members who were to be selected by banks. After hearing from Bryan and Owen and consulting with Brandeis, Wilson insisted that the Federal Reserve Board be made up *exclusively* of public members. It is unclear whether a Board made up partially of private bankers would make different decisions than a board consisting solely of public members. Likely, they generally would come out about the same. However, as in most political matters, the issue was not one of differences in results, but rather of appearances. Aldrich and his advisers may have been geniuses when it came to the mechanics of central banking. They were clueless when it came to devising a reserve banking law that could garner the support of the American people and Congress. Brandeis and Wilson were far wiser in insisting on exclusive public control, and Glass was wise to accede to them.

In short, the technical portions of the act, which comprise the vast majority of its provisions, were based on the Aldrich Plan. The political aspects of the act, decentralization and public control, came from Glass and Wilson.

There is an obvious question—if most of the act was based on the Aldrich Plan, why did Glass and Willis on one hand, and Aldrich on the other, insist that this was not the case? The answer comes down to classic partisan politics. Democrats like Glass and Willis were not about to admit that they borrowed heavily from a Republican scheme. On the other hand, a dyed-in-the-wool Republican like Aldrich wanted to criticize the Democrats' bill, not say that it was based on his bill. It brings to mind Glass's belief that Republican senator Henry Cabot Lodge opposed Senate approval of the Treaty of Versailles because of pure partisan politics. Glass said that if Republican president Theodore Roosevelt, rather than Democrat Wilson, had sponsored the treaty, "Lodge and his entire outfit would have hailed it as a brilliant performance and would have gulped it down without the dotting of an i or the crossing of a t."[57]

Steering the Act Through Congress

As we have seen, the Federal Reserve Act had a long and torturous legislative history. James Livingston has referred to "the insanely complicated struggles over the various drafts of banking legislation that eventually emerged from congressional committees in 1913."[58]

Many individuals played critical roles in obtaining congressional approval of this highly complex and controversial measure. President Wilson provided overall presidential leadership and intervened at key moments. Secretary of State Bryan quelled strong agrarian opposition to the legislation; Bryan literally was the only person in the nation who could have had such a decisive impact. Glass must have been delighted when writers on the act credited him as the key political player. In 1938, Professor George W. Edwards wrote that "Leadership in the [banking reform] movement was taken by the Banking and Currency Committee of the House of Representatives of which Carter Glass was the dominant figure." That same year, Alexander Dana Noyes wrote that the act "made the national reputation of the congressman who, more than any public man,—not excepting the president, whose attitude throughout the controversy was conservative and correct,—brought to success the remarkable legislative undertaking."[59]

These writers were correct. Glass was the most important political actor. He prepared a complete reserve banking bill *before* Woodrow Wilson was elected president. He drafted his bill to provide a unique, decentralized system, while borrowing many technical provisions from the Aldrich Plan. He accepted changes from allies and fought off adversaries. Throughout the long process, Glass demonstrated tenacity and "pluck" in striving to obtain agreement on reasonable reserve banking legislation, while tacking and compromising as necessary. Humorist Will Rogers was correct when he wrote, "When they get all through arguing over 'Who is the Father of the Federal Reserve Act' why they will really find the sire to be none other than Carter Glass."[60]

4

THE ROARING 20s: GLASS'S WARNINGS GO UNHEEDED

The immense amount of these [brokers'] loans constitutes a direct menace to sound commercial transactions and betokes a perfect spirit of speculation, the very thing against which federal reserve legislation was directed.

—Carter Glass

In 1918, President Wilson appointed Glass Secretary of the Treasury. The following year, the governor of Virginia named him to an open seat in the United States Senate, to which he was subsequently was elected four times. In the late 1920s, Glass became increasingly concerned that regional Federal Reserve Banks were facilitating the huge flow of money from across the country to Wall Street speculators, making a stock market crash inevitable. Glass urged the Federal Reserve Board to take action to stem the flow, but his warnings were largely ignored.

Glass as Secretary of the Treasury

In 1912, Glass had supported Woodrow Wilson's successful effort to gain the Democratic presidential nomination because, as governor

8. The New Secretary of the Treasury Going to Work, Washington *Evening Star*, 1918.

of New Jersey, Wilson had opposed the Democratic machine and corporate influence. Glass's dealings with President Wilson during the long battle for the Federal Reserve Act increased his admiration. Glass came to believe that Wilson was "the greatest Christian statesman of all time."[1] In addition to spearheading the drive for the Federal Reserve Act, Glass voted for all of the Wilson Administration's other major laws, including the Underwood Tariff, the Clayton Act, the Federal Trade Commission Act, and the Federal Farm Loan Act.

Wilson reciprocated Glass's loyalty. In 1916, at Wilson's request,

Glass was named Secretary of the Democratic National Committee and helped draft the party's platform.[2] There were press reports that Wilson would appoint Glass to the Federal Reserve Board.[3] However, in November 1918, William G. McAdoo announced that he intended to resign as Secretary of the Treasury. President Wilson nominated Glass to fill the position. Glass was confirmed by the Senate without opposition.

The United States had financed the costs of the First World War largely through the sale of U.S. government bonds in small denominations to the public. This was the first time that many Americans invested in securities. "Whereas [in 1899] less than 1 percent of the population owned stocks or bonds ... approximately one-third of the population (34 million Americans) purchased some form of federal bond during World War I."[4]

Glass's first major task as Secretary of the Treasury was to oversee efforts to sell $5 billion worth of Victory Bonds to the general public. Now that the war had ended and patriotic feelings had ebbed, there was widespread doubt that the public would finance an entire issue of this size: "From all sides, within and without the Cabinet, the Congress, and Wall Street, Glass was told it was hopeless to attempt to sell the needed $5,000,000,000 in Victory Bonds."[5] The American Bankers Association urged Glass to cut the public offering in half and place the remaining issue of Victory Bonds with private banks.

As might have been expected, given Glass's reputation for tenacity and "pluck," these warnings only increased his desire to sell the entire $5 billion issue directly to the public. Glass travelled across the country to encourage Americans both to fulfill their patriotic duty and to make sound investments. He also urged regional Federal Reserve Banks to encourage commercial banks to cooperate in the sales campaign. Glass's efforts were successful. The Victory Bond offering was oversubscribed.

Increased Suspicions About Wall Street

Glass's experiences as Secretary of the Treasury increased his suspicions about Wall Street, suspicions that had first been aroused when he was a newspaper editor in the 1890s, fighting for currency backed by silver.

During the First World War, Congress had created the Capital Issues Committee, which was made up of representatives from the Treasury Department, Federal Reserve, and the banking industry, and which had the authority to determine whether proposed offerings of corporate securities were compatible with the war effort. After the war, when the committee was disbanding, its chairman called for the enactment of permanent federal securities legislation. Secretary of the Treasury Glass stated that he intended to "ask Congress immediately for legislation that will check the traffic in worthless securities while imposing no undue restrictions upon the financing of legitimate business."[6]

Soon thereafter, Glass learned that some New York securities firms wanted to persuade investors to *sell* their U.S. government bonds and invest the proceeds in new issues of corporate securities that were being underwritten by these firms. Glass struck back by having a bill, entitled the Federal Stock Publicity Act, drafted by the Capital Issues Committee.[7] The bill would have required any firm selling corporate shares to the public to prepare and file a detailed financial statement with the Treasury Department, including information regarding stock ownership by officers and directors; classes of outstanding securities; proceeds from recent offerings of the corporation's securities; the identity of the underwriters and their fees; the use of proceeds from the new offering; and the issuer's accounting firms and their reports. Every prospectus, advertisement, or other communication relating to the offering would have to mention that the statement was on file at the Treasury Department where it would have to be open to public inspection. The issuer would have to offer to send a copy to any person free of charge upon request. If a statement was false in any material respect, any purchaser of the shares would have the right to rescind the transaction and receive back the purchase price.

The bill was introduced in Congress by Representative Thomas Taylor, a Democrat from Colorado.[8] Introduction of the legislation caused the New York securities firms to drop their efforts to persuade investors to sell government bonds and invest in new corporate securities. The bill did not receive support from the Wilson Administration, which was preoccupied with the battle over U. S. membership in the League of Nations. Legislation regarding public offerings of securities was not enacted until passage of the Securities Act of 1933, discussed in Chapter 8.

Glass's experience as Secretary of the Treasury also led him to see the need to reform the New York Stock Exchange. An October 25, 1919, exchange of memoranda between Glass and Assistant Secretary of the Treasury Russell Leffingwell stated: "Although the New York Stock Exchange furnishes a valuable and necessary safety valve and barometer, its methods must be reformed so as to suppress manipulation and also as to the settlement and financing of transactions. These reforms should, of course, come from within. But if the Exchange cannot or will not reform itself then sooner or later the Government must undertake the task."[9] As discussed in Chapter 8, it was not until 1934 that Congress enacted the Securities Exchange Act providing for federal oversight of the nation's securities exchanges.

Finally, when he served as Secretary of the Treasury, Glass worried about market speculation fueled by excessive amounts of credit extended by commercial banks to investors and speculators. He was concerned that this activity was diverting credit away from the legitimate needs of regional businesses and government to Wall Street, one concern that had led him in 1913 to devise the decentralized reserve banking system in the Federal Reserve Act. Glass knew that one way to address this problem would be for the Fed to raise the discount rate (the rate that Federal Reserve Banks charged commercial banks for their borrowings). However, doing so would have an adverse impact on all borrowers, not just securities investors. Therefore, the Fed instead agreed to monitor member bank lending policies and encourage them to reduce securities lending.[10]

Appointment to the Senate

In late 1919, Virginia governor Westmoreland Davis offered Glass the opportunity to fill the United States Senate seat of Thomas S. Martin, who had died. Accepting the seat would require Glass to resign as Secretary of the Treasury. President Wilson urged Glass to leave the Treasury Department to take the seat, probably because this would strengthen Wilson's chances of obtaining his number one wish—Senate approval of the Treaty of Versailles and U.S. membership in the League of Nations.[11] Glass agreed to accept the appointment. As one writer, Chester B. Goolrick, Jr., has observed, Glass was so devoted to Wilson that he "probably would have cheerfully cut off his ears had Wilson so ordered."[12] On November 15, 1919, Governor Davis appointed Glass to the Senate.

Glass's early time in the Senate was largely devoted to working, unsuccessfully, for Senate ratification of the Treaty of Versailles and United States membership in the League of Nations. Goolrick noted, "Defeat and bitterness marked his early years in the Senate; there were times when, rallying 'round the Wilson standard, he found himself virtually without allies on the battlefield."[13] Opposition to the treaty and U.S. membership in the league was led by Republican Senator Henry Cabot Lodge, chairman of the Senate Foreign Relations Committee. Glass was convinced that Lodge's position was based on political opportunism and personal hatred of Wilson.

It undoubtedly was with a sense of relief that Glass turned from the battle over U.S. membership in the League of Nations to defending the Federal Reserve System that he had helped create in 1913. During the long and arduous process that led to the enactment of the

Federal Reserve Act, Glass had encountered two main opponents to his attempt to create a balanced and decentralized system—agrarian members of Congress who feared that the system actually was a disguised central bank and representatives of big city commercial banks who wanted to control the system. In the 1920s, these groups tried to change the functioning of the Federal Reserve System to their advantage. Glass opposed both groups.

Agrarians and the Federal Reserve System

Prices for agricultural products rose sharply during the First World War. This led farmers to borrow heavily in order to purchase more land and equipment. Farm production and farm exports soared. Farmers prospered. However, when the war ended, farm prices collapsed. Wheat that sold for $2.56 a bushel in June 1920 fell to $1.03 in August 1921. Cotton that sold for 41 cents a pound in July 1920 fell to 12 cents in June 1921. Corn went from $1.85 a bushel in June 1920 to 42 cents at the end of 1921. While farm income plummeted, farm debt increased.[14] Farm organizations and members of Congress from the agrarian south and west blamed the Federal Reserve System for their problems. They alleged that the Federal Reserve Board had raised the discount rate on loans secured by agricultural land and products, withholding money from country banks in order to supply big city banks with money for speculation.

Glass vigorously opposed giving farmers special treatment under the Federal Reserve Act. In particular, he believed that the Federal Reserve System should not be used to try to set the prices of farm products. In 1922, Senator Arthur Clapper, a Republican from Kansas, introduced legislation authorizing the creation of private agricultural credit corporations, which could issue commercial paper with up to nine months' maturities that would be eligible for discount by Federal Reserve Banks. Glass blasted the bill's sponsors for alleging that the Federal Reserve System was in any way to blame for the decline in farm prices. He opposed changing the Federal Reserve System into a mechanism to assist specific segments of the economy, be they farmers or manufacturers, labeling such policies as "legalized pillage."[15]

Glass was sympathetic to farmers' plight. However, he believed that farmers' problems resulted from overproduction and not from inadequate access to credit. He thought that the solution lay in farmers establishing cooperative marketing corporations that could store agricultural products and release them to the markets at opportune times. He wrote to one Virginia citizen, "I have repeatedly in letters, some of which have been published, strongly advocated sane organization by farmers on business principles to insure orderly marketing of their crops."[16] In a letter to another Virginian, he was more specific:

> The real trouble with the American farmer is the disorderly fashion in which crops are produced and marketed. Every other industry is so organized as to regulate production in accord with the demand; and until farmers cooperate effectively in the same way they will find themselves at a disadvantage. It is for this reason that I so earnestly favor the orderly marketing of crops, such as has prevailed on the Eastern Shore of Virginia for so many years and later among the fruit growers of California and is now attempted by the cotton and tobacco farmers of the South.[17]

Glass's battles with agricultural interests were nothing compared to his fights with Wall Street.

Wall Street and the Federal Reserve System

Glass and Willis were believers in the "real bills" doctrine, under which a public or private central banking authority should only discount loans made by commercial banks for trade and agriculture, not for speculation in commodities or corporate securities. This doctrine was reflected in the Federal Reserve Act's wording concerning the activities of the regional Federal Reserve Banks. Glass stated that one of his principal goals in working for the decentralized Federal Reserve System had been "to break down the artificial connection between the banking business of this country, and the stock speculative operations at the money centers."[18] However, in the 1920s, Glass came to believe that weak leadership of the Federal Reserve System facilitated this very abuse—the massive movement of funds from around the country to Wall Street to finance stock speculation.

The stock market boomed in the mid- to late-1920s. A diversified portfolio of common stocks would have more than tripled in value from June 1924 to September 1929. The boom was fueled in part by investors borrowing from their brokers to purchase shares, a practice commonly termed "buying on margin." Banks lent money to brokers so that the brokers, in turn, could provide margin loans to investors. Professor Robert Sobel has observed, "At the beginning of the decade, there were approximately $1 billion in such [brokers'] loans outstanding. By early 1926 ... they had risen to $2.5 billion. Two years later the figure was $3.5 billion.... by January 1, 1929, call loans were well over $6 billion. By early October 1929 more than $8.5 billion in loans were outstanding."[19]

The money for brokers' loans came from a number of sources. In the first instance, New York commercial banks lent money to securities firms. Second, commercial banks from around the country lent money to New York banks, who, in turn, lent it to securities firms. Third, wealthy individuals, foreign concerns, and American corporations lent increasing amounts of money to New York banks. Finally, as John Kenneth Galbraith noted, "In principle, New York banks could borrow money from the Federal Reserve Bank for 5 per cent and re-lend it in the call market for 12. In practice, they did. This was, possibly, the most profitable arbitrage operation of all time."[20]

Glass's worst nightmare was taking place: the Federal Reserve Banks that he had helped create in order to maintain a *decentralized* financial system were *facilitating* the huge flow of money from across the nation to Wall Street speculators. Galbraith wrote that as a result of these various sources of funds for margin lending, "a great river of gold began to converge on Wall Street, all of it to help Americans hold common stock on margin."[21]

Federal Reserve Board officials were well aware of the stock market boom, the extraordinary increase in brokers' loans, and the indirect financing of many of those loans by Federal Reserve Banks. There were a number of steps the board could have taken to stop, or at least slow, these developments:

- The board could have asked Congress for authority to set margin requirements. (In the 1920s, there were no government-imposed margin limits; brokers set their own margin limits.)
- A board official could have given a speech denouncing stock market speculation and warning that the stock market was overpriced.
- The board could have raised the discount rate that Federal Reserve Banks charged commercial banks, thus requiring the banks to increase the interest rates that they, in turn, charged securities firms that were financing investors' margin accounts.

Each of these measures had possible downsides. Imposing, or even proposing to impose, margin requirements, or delivering a warning speech, could set off a panic. Raising the discount rate would increase the costs of agricultural and business loans, not just loans on securities. However, inaction meant that stock prices, purchases of stock on margin, and the flow of money from across the nation to Wall Street was likely to increase. Under weak leadership and with little experience, the board declined to do anything. Galbraith went so far as to suggest willful negligence: "the Federal Reserve was helpless only because it wanted to be."[22]

As discussed in Chapters 1 and 3, Glass's upbringing in the post–Civil War South had made him wary of northern financial interests, and he created a decentralized reserve banking system precisely to prevent Wall Street control. In January 1928, Glass wrote to one correspondent, "I think the immense amount of these [brokers'] loans constitutes a distinct menace to sound commercial transactions and betokes a perfect spirit of speculation, the very thing against which federal reserve legislation was directed." In April, Glass wrote to another correspondent:

> Among the primary reasons for the Federal Reserve Act was the purpose to withhold from speculative uses the reserve funds of the country. We had supposed that this might have a salutary effect in persuading interior banks to give local enterprises, whether industrial or commercial, the benefit of the natural law of supply and demand.... To some of us it seems not only unnatural, but positively unfair, that the money made in a given community, as well as the credits created, should not be used to stimulate the business interests of that given community rather than sent off to New York, to be used in purely non-productive stock and commodity gambling."[23]

In February and March of 1928, the Senate Committee on Banking and Currency held hearings on brokers' loans. Following the hearings, Senator Robert M. La Follette, a Progressive from Wisconsin, introduced a resolution requiring the Federal Reserve Board to admonish Federal Reserve Banks to advise member banks against further expansion of loans for speculative purposes. The resolution also would have required the board to report to Congress as to what legislation, if any, was required to prevent excessive use of Federal Reserve System funds and credits for speculation.

Glass hoped that the threat of legislation would finally cause the Federal Reserve Board to act. He wrote an article in which he stated that brokers' loans were a "departure from the spirit and intention of the Federal Reserve Act," and that the "sucking in of the country's resources for use in gambling in stocks and bonds ... is precisely the sort of thing the Federal Reserve Act was designed to prevent, or at least to minimize." He was convinced that the board had ample authority to direct the policies of the regional Federal Reserve Banks to lessen stock speculation. Specifically, Glass wanted the board to order Federal Reserve Banks to refuse requests for rediscount of loans from member banks if the Reserve Banks thought that the proceeds were going to be used to finance speculation.[24]

Glass wrote to Federal Reserve Board member Edmund Platt, "I have not the remotest doubt that the Federal Reserve Board could admonish federal reserve banks against the unreserved policy of permitting the facilities of the system to be used in this way and could do it effectively. Should any federal reserve bank refuse to respect the admonition, its officials should be summarily removed."[25]

The pressure exerted by Glass and other senators finally had an impact on the board. It raised the discount rate three times. However, these moves did not work. Although Fed member banks reduced their call loan commitments, new money for brokers' loans came from wealthy individuals and corporations, over whom the Federal Reserve Board had no direct control.[26]

At last, on February 2, 1929, the board moved in the direction Glass had urged by telling the regional Reserve Banks that it was not reasonable for a commercial bank to seek to rediscount at a Reserve Bank any loan made to finance speculation:

A member [bank] is not within its reasonable claims for

re-discount facilities at its reserve bank when it borrows for the purpose of making speculative loans or for the purpose of maintaining speculative loans. The board has no disposition to assume authority or interfere with the loan practices of member banks, so long as they do not involve the Federal reserve banks. It has, however, a grave responsibility whenever there is evidence that member banks are maintaining speculative security loans with the aid of Federal reserve credit.[27]

Five days later, the board repeated its position:

When [the Board] finds that conditions are arising which obstruct the Federal reserve banks in the effective discharge of their functions of so managing the credit facilities of the Federal reserve system as to accommodate commerce and business, it is its duty to inquire into them and to take such measures as may be deemed suitable and effective in the circumstances to correct them; which, in their immediate situation, means to restrain the use, either directly or indirectly, of Federal Reserve facilities in aid of the growth of speculative credit.[28]

These pronouncements by the board produced two very different reactions. On the one hand, Glass felt that the board's statements did not go nearly far enough since they did not *explicitly* order Federal Reserve Banks not to rediscount commercial paper from banks if they thought that the proceeds would be used to finance speculation. On the other hand, Charles E. Mitchell, chairman of the board of the National City Bank of New York and a director of the Federal Reserve Bank of New York, was defiant. On March 26, 1929, Mitchell declared that, despite the board's pronouncements, his bank would continue to present commercial paper to the New York Reserve

Bank for rediscount and would use the proceeds to finance brokers' loans. The next day, he put his bank's money where his mouth was: National City announced that it would provide $25 million to New York brokers. Mitchell's statement and actions were a direct slap at the board, but it did not respond.[29]

Glass was incensed. He concluded that Mitchell was more loyal to the stock market than to his obligations as a director of the New York Federal Reserve Bank. He felt that unless Mitchell accepted the Federal Reserve Board's position, he should be fired from his directorship at the New York Federal Reserve Bank.[30] However, neither the New York Federal Reserve Bank nor the Federal Reserve Board in Washington, DC did anything to bring Mitchell into line.

Glass was now becoming more concerned than ever. He worried that the excessive level of brokers' loans made a stock market crash inevitable. He feared that so much speculative money was pouring into Wall Street that legitimate businesses were being required to pay higher interest rates on their borrowings. He believed that states and communities were deferring issuing bonds because of the high interest rates they would have to pay. Glass wrote a letter to the *New York Times* stating that he wanted to reduce the level of securities speculation not because of the "wickedness" of stock gambling, but because of his concern about "the economic integrity of the Federal Reserve banking system."[31]

With a great deal of foresight, Glass put forth concrete proposals to slow speculation and buying on margin. He continued to urge that Federal Reserve Banks refuse to rediscount commercial paper if they believed the proceeds would be used for speculation. He called for repealing the section of the Federal Reserve Act that permitted commercial banks to borrow for fifteen days on U.S. government bonds. He recommended legislation imposing a five per cent tax on stock purchases held for less than sixty days.[32]

Glass's warnings not only went unheeded. They were scoffed at. A *Wall Street Journal* editorial mocked Glass for confusing "speculation" with "gambling." The *Journal* contended that "the difference ... is in the consideration. In a speculative transaction there is a genuine transfer of something of value as, for instance, a piece of mortgaged real estate.... In a gambling transaction, like a bet, there is no consideration." The *Journal* concluded, "if Senators gave the matter more thought and less talk they would add to their usefulness."[33] A *New York Herald* editorial stated that "some interesting and unusual ideas of finance are current in the greatest deliberative body in the world," giving as an example Glass's criticism of corporations lending money for speculation rather than paying dividends to stockholders. The *Herald* opined, "the chances are that most stockholders will profit ... at least for the time being."[34]

In a cruel irony Glass was ridiculed in a book written in mid-1929 by an economics professor at Princeton, the university that had been headed by Glass's hero, Woodrow Wilson. In his June 10, 1929, preface to *Washington and Wall Street,* Professor Joseph Stagg Lawrence criticized senators for their concerns over stock market speculation:

> During the past week the nation has been treated to the diverting but pathetic spectacle of the "most august" legislative chamber on earth gone berserk on the subject of speculation. It seems incredible that in the year of our Grace 1929 a body of presumably intelligent public men should permit fanatical passions and provincial ignorance to find expression in unrestrained virulence. Yet that is precisely what has taken place. It is impossible to dignify these wanton attacks on the financial community as discussions. Such a term implies reason and restraint.[35]

Professor Lawrence went on to single out Glass: "When the Senator from the Old Dominion rose in that chamber of absurdities, sometimes referred to as a deliberative assembly, his remarks were characterized by neither reason nor restraint. Blatant bigotry and turbulent provincialism have joined to condemn an innocent community."

Professor Lawrence took another shot at Glass, who had worked tirelessly for United States' membership in the League of Nations, by lumping him in with senators who had blocked U.S. membership: "This identical group has given us prohibition. It has prevented our participation in the League of Nations. It has discovered farm relief. Now it is revealing the hideous turpitude of Wall Street."

Professor Lawrence specifically criticized Glass's proposal to slow speculation through a tax on short-term trading: "The five percent tax on sales assuming no method of evasion could be discovered would be disastrous not only to stock brokers but to all industry including the farmer. It would paralyze the exchanges and vitally impair one of the most important rights of ownership, the right of unconditional disposal. It would be worse than confiscation since the latter yields a revenue to the state whereas this restriction would destroy values without any compensating gains to any one. Vandalism describes the act better than confiscation.... Its application would fall upon our fair land like the blight of disaster."[36]

Glass's fears over the likely consequences of excessive speculation, fueled by brokers' loans and the passivity of the Federal Reserve Board, were borne out by the great stock market crash in October 1929. Glass thought that there was plenty of blame to go around, but he singled out Charles E. Mitchell, president of the National City Bank, who Glass said, "more than any fifty men, is responsible for the crash."[37]

As to Professor Lawrence, John Kenneth Galbraith wryly noted that after the crash, "Mr. Lawrence disappeared from Princeton. Among economists his voice was not heard again."[38]

On the other hand, the events of October 1929 prepared the way for Glass to begin work on his second major legislative accomplishment, the Glass-Steagall Act.

5
POST-1929 CRASH:
GLASS'S BANKING REFORM BILL

Once you begin the dance of legislation,
you must struggle through its mazes as best you can
to the breathless end—if any end there be.

—President Woodrow Wilson

Following the 1929 crash, the Republican–controlled Congress named Glass, a Democrat, to chair a subcommittee to address bank involvement in securities speculation. Glass drafted a bill limiting bank loans to financial firms, prohibiting banks borrowing from Federal Reserve Banks to finance brokers' loans, prohibiting banks from engaging in securities activities, and subjecting securities firms controlled by banks ("security affiliates") to regulation. Glass subsequently amended the bill to prohibit security affiliates. As the Hoover Administration ended, Glass obtained Senate approval of the bill, but the House did not act.

Appointment of the Glass Subcommittee

In May 1929, Senator William H. King, a Democrat from Utah, introduced a resolution directing the Senate Banking Committee to investigate the Federal Reserve System, particularly commercial banks' involvement with speculative securities activities. Not surprisingly, in the midst of the stock market boom of the late 1920s, the Senate did not act on King's resolution. In October 1929, the stock market crashed, ushering in the Great Depression. After the crash, Glass introduced a revised resolution that called for an investigation into a wide range of topics relating to the national and Federal Reserve banking systems: (1) "the administration of these banking systems with respect to the use of their facilities for trading in and carrying speculative securities"; (2) "the extent of call loans to brokers by member banks for such purposes"; (3) "the effect on the systems of the formulation of investment and security trusts"; (4) "the desirability of chain banking"; (5) "the development of branch banking as part of the national system"; and (6) "any related problems which the committee may think it important to investigate." The crash had changed everything. The Senate adopted the revised resolution in May 1930 without debate and without a record vote.[1]

Although the Senate was controlled by Republicans, the chairman of the Banking Committee, Senator Norbeck of North Dakota, named Glass, a Democrat, to head the subcommittee that would conduct the investigation. This was an indication of the bipartisan respect accorded to Glass on banking issues.

Glass hired Dr. H. Parker Willis, who had worked with Glass on the Federal Reserve Act and was now a professor of economics at Columbia University, as chief adviser to the subcommittee. A research staff was assembled, and work began on pursuing an exhaustive investigation. Helen Burns wrote, "The work undertaken constituted the most comprehensive investigation of the general banking situation since that done by the National Monetary Commission in 1908."[2]

At the outset, Glass had a major choice—he could seek to develop a completely new system of American banking (for example, unifying the existing federal and forty-eight-state banking systems into a single system under the Federal Reserve Board and permitting statewide or even nation-wide branching), or he could instead address deficiencies in the existing multiple systems. Willis later wrote that

Glass and the subcommittee decided to adopt the latter "patching up" approach and pursue "a remedial rather than a constructive" law because of political factors. Glass and Willis were convinced that a banking law could only be enacted if it had the approval of the Hoover Administration or was so popular that it couldn't be blocked by the administration. They viewed President Hoover, Secretary of the Treasury Mills, and the Republican majorities in both houses of congress as unfavorably disposed to major banking reform legislation.[3]

As set forth in his resolution, a major area that Glass and the subcommittee were to consider were the securities activities conducted by commercial banking organizations. This included both securities activities conducted *directly* by banks and securities activities conducted by securities firms related to banks, so-called bank "security affiliates." At this point, it is appropriate to provide background information on bank security affiliates since they were to become a major point of controversy in the development of Glass's banking reform legislation.

In the late nineteenth century, state-chartered trust companies began to engage both in traditional commercial banking activities, such as taking deposits and making commercial loans, and in the distribution and sale of securities. Many national banks in major financial centers wanted to engage in similar types of securities activities. However, the National Banking Act was interpreted as generally prohibiting national banks from *directly* engaging in most securities activities. Therefore, beginning in 1908, many national banks formed separate companies known as "security affiliates" to perform securities activities. Banks and their security affiliates were commonly joined in two ways: the bank and its security affiliate employed common officers and directors, and they issued stock certificates that evidenced ownership of shares in both the bank and its security affiliate. In 1920, the Comptroller of the Currency pointed out potential abuses resulting from the operation of security affiliates by national banks and recommended that Congress enact appropriate legislation. However, later in the 1920s, the Comptroller's attitude reversed. He became the driving force behind legislation that expanded national banks' authority to engage in securities activities.[4] In the late 1920s, large national banks through their security affiliates became the dominant force in investment banking, alongside traditional private investment banking firms such as J. P. Morgan & Co. and Kuhn, Loeb & Company.

In January 1930, Willis authored an article in which he discussed three areas: (1) Willis criticized commercial bank loans made for the purpose of enabling securities firms to underwrite or guarantee securities; (2) Willis was emphatic that "It will be necessary ... to get the national banks and, so far as possible, the state banks also out of the investment banking business"; and (3) Willis expressed concern over commercial bank loans to their security affiliates, stating that in many instances, "bank lendings to affiliated security companies have gone far beyond the limits of prudence and safety." Willis did *not* call for separating banks and their security affiliates as the Pujo subcommittee and Louis Brandeis had done in 1913, or for generally regulating security affiliates. Instead, he only called for unspecified "controls" to be imposed on "the lending relations between banks and affiliated security companies."[5]

Glass's subcommittee initially considered three ways to address bank security affiliates: (1) subject the affiliates to federal regulation, presumably by federal banking regulators, the Comptroller of the Currency, and the Federal Reserve Board; (2) require the affiliates to be chartered under new federal laws (presumably the chartering requirements would impose standards); or (3) require the separation of security affiliates from their associated banks. The subcommittee quickly rejected the federal chartering approach since it would take a long time to develop and thus would delay action on the entire bill. Therefore, the subcommittee's choice was between subjecting bank security affiliates to federal regulation or requiring the separation of commercial banks and their security affiliates.[6]

Glass's First Bill: Regulation of Bank Security Affiliates

In June 1930, Glass and Willis prepared a draft bill, S. 4723, designed to help guide the subcommittee's investigation.[7] Glass's main concern was the same as it had been in the late 1920s—banks' extensions of credit, particularly through use of Federal Reserve Banks, to fuel stock market speculation. Two sections of the draft bill addressed this issue. First, Section 6 limited the amount that a national bank could lend to brokers, stock exchange members, finance companies, securities companies, investment trusts, and bank affiliates to 10 percent of the bank's capital. Second, Section 11 prohibited a member bank from borrowing from a Federal Reserve Bank on legitimate commercial paper and using the proceeds to finance loans to brokers.

The final banking reform legislation that was enacted in 1933, the Glass-Steagall Act, was to become famous for two types of provisions. First, it provided for federal insurance of bank deposits, and second, it required the separation of banks and their security affiliates. Glass's first bill was quite different from the final Glass-Steagall Act in both areas.

First, Glass's initial bill did not provide for any type of deposit insurance. There were many calls for federal insurance of deposits. However, as Willis explained, "Chairman Glass had never believed in the efficacy of this expedient," and therefore he did not include it in his first bill.[8]

Second, Glass's initial bill made the same distinction between banks and bank security affiliates that Willis had made in his article in January 1930. Section 2 sharply limited the securities activities that could be conducted directly by national banks to acting solely as uninterested brokers for customers: "the business of buying and selling investment securities shall hereafter be limited to buying and selling without recourse, and solely upon order, and for the account of customers, and in no case for its own account." Thus, national banks could not underwrite new issues of securities or buy and sell securities for their own accounts. In contrast, Sections 7 and 9 did not limit or end the activities of bank security affiliates, but only required security affiliates of national banks to file reports with the Comptroller of the Currency and security affiliates of state-chartered banks that were members of the Federal Reserve System to file reports with the Fed. The final Glass-Steagall Act was to become famous for its use of a "fragmentation" approach, requiring separation of banks and their security affiliates. However, Glass's initial bill utilized a more traditional "regulatory" approach.[9]

The subcommittee held hearings in January, February, and March 1931 at which the Comptroller of the Currency, representatives of the Federal Reserve System and Federal Reserve Banks, state bank regulators, and bank executives, testified.[10] Many witnesses addressed provisions in the bill that dealt with bank loans to securities firms and with bank security affiliates. On the second day of the hearings, Glass expressed his own view regarding the treatment of bank security affiliates, "If it is not possible to control them in some way, I should be agreeable to prohibiting them."[11]

Hanging over the subcommittee's hearing room was the very recent failure, in December 1930, of a major New York State–chartered bank, the Bank of the United States, the fourth largest bank in New York City. Many of the bank's over 400,000 depositors believed, erroneously, that the bank's name meant that it was connected to the United States government. The bank's president, Bernard Marcus, had used the bank's funds for his personal speculative activities and had done so through the creation of fifty-nine affiliates of the bank (none of which was a security affiliate.) The *New York Times* reported, "Long queues of depositors formed at the doors of a few of the branch banks.... [At] several of the branches there were pitiful scenes as women depositors, unable to get inside, besieged the police guards for explanation and help."[12]

The failure of the Bank of the United States received widespread coverage in the press, with many people claiming that the failure was because of the affiliate system. At the Glass subcommittee's hearings, senators and Professor Willis asked witness after witness about the failure of the Bank of the United States and its relevance to legislation regarding bank security affiliates.[13]

Government witnesses offered a wide range of views regarding bank loans for securities speculation and bank security affiliates. The Comptroller of the Currency, J. W. Pole, generally defended brokers' loans, and stated that legislation was needed to limit the aggregate amount a bank could lend to its security affiliate. George L. Harrison, a governor of the New York Federal Reserve Bank, testified that the proper way to restrict brokers' loans was to raise the rediscount rate for *all* commercial loans. He supported new laws giving regulators the authority to examine bank security affiliates. Harrison also favored prohibiting a bank from purchasing securities from its security affiliate. Arthur C. Miller, a member of the Federal Reserve Board, testified that bank security affiliates created major problems: "If we had not had these affiliated institutions in 1928 and 1929, we should not have had as bad a situation, speculatively, as we have had…. By reason of their access to the credit facilities of the banks with which they are affiliated, and the access of the banks to the Federal reserve system, it has been made very easy for investment affiliates to spread into dangerous zones." As to the legislative solution, Miller preferred ending bank ties to security affiliates, but since it was difficult to "unscramble" the existing relationships, he supported strict regulation of security affiliates.[14]

Perhaps the most important testimony was given by John Broderick, Superintendent of Banking for the State of New York. At the time of his appearance before the subcommittee, Broderick was heavily involved in the fallout of the recent failure of the Bank of the United States, which was widely attributed to the bank's numerous affiliates. Broderick testified that he was recommending legislation to the New

York State legislature providing first, that an officer of a New York–chartered bank could not serve as an officer or director of a securities firm, and second, that stock certificates of a New York-chartered bank could not simultaneously represent stock in another company, including any affiliate. These two steps would effectively separate New York State–chartered banks and their security affiliates. Moreover, Broderick recommended that private investment banks be prohibited from accepting deposits, thus ending their linkage to routine commercial banking.[15]

Report Detailing Problems of Bank Security Affiliates

Glass, aided by Willis, prepared a report summarizing the subcommittee's conclusions concerning the relationship of banks with the security markets, although it did not make recommendations for legislation. Two areas merit special attention.

First, given Glass's long-standing concern over bank loans used to finance securities investments, it is not surprising that the first part of the report was devoted to this matter. Glass was convinced that there was a substantial difference between commercial loans, which tended to be self-liquidating, and securities loans, whose liquidity depended on brokerage firms' ability to sell their customers' securities collateral at a price that would cover the loan. A sharp decline in securities prices could force investors and their brokers to sell substantial amounts of collateral into the markets, further depressing securities prices. Moreover, a bank's loans to brokerage firms lessened its ability to lend to other business borrowers beyond the financial sector.[16]

Second, the report focused on bank security affiliates. Previously Glass's and Willis's concern in this area had been limited to banks' lending to their security affiliates. The report reflected this concern, stating that activities of a bank's security affiliate as a holding or finance company or an investment trust are also fraught with the danger of large losses during a deflation period. Bank affiliates of this kind show a much greater tendency to operate with borrowed funds than do organizations of this type which are independent of banks, the reason being the identity of control and management which prevails between the bank and its affiliate tends to encourage reliance upon the lending facilities of the former.[17]

However, the report then went well beyond the lending issue. It enumerated numerous *other* ways in which operations of a bank security affiliate could affect the position and soundness of the bank, with an emphasis on negative effects:

(2) The affiliate may sell securities to the bank ... or vice versa.

(3) The bank is closely connected in the public mind with its affiliates, and should the latter suffer large losses it is practically unthinkable that they should be allowed to fail. Instead, the bank would normally support it by additional loans or other aid, thus becoming more deeply involved itself. The knowledge that the affiliate has suffered large losses may in itself be sufficient to cause unfavorable rumors, however unjustified, about the bank.

(4) The bank, to relieve the affiliate of excess holdings, may purchase securities from it.

(5) The bank may lend much more freely to customers on issues sponsored by the securities affiliate, in order to facilitate their distribution, than it would otherwise do.

(6) The good will of the bank with its depositors may be adversely affected to a serious degree when the latter suffer substantial losses on security issues purchased from the affiliate.

(7) Operations by the affiliate in the market for the bank's own stock may cause undesirably wide fluctuations in

the latter.

(8) Wide variations in the net asset value, earning power, and dividend-paying ability of security affiliates tend to make bank stock fluctuations much greater than would otherwise be the case.

(9) The existence of the affiliates may induce the bank to make unwise commitments, in the knowledge that in case of need they can be shifted to the affiliates, and thus be removed from the bank's condition statement.

(10) Knowing its access to the resources of the bank in case of need, security affiliates in their turn may tend to assume various commitments less cautiously than do private investment banking houses.

(11) In the case of a trust company or a bank with a trust department, the possession of a security affiliate may adversely affect the independence with which fiduciary activities are exercised.[18]

This extensive listing of problems with bank security affiliates gave an indication that Glass had come to believe that federal regulation of bank security affiliates, as provided in his first bill, might not be sufficient, and therefore that separation might be required.

The report also demonstrated that the failure of the Bank of the United States and its numerous affiliates had registered with Glass's subcommittee. The final paragraph of the section in the report on bank security affiliates stated: "In New York State, where most of the large security affiliates are to be found, sentiment on the subject was aroused among bankers, as well as the general public, by the effects of the stock market deflation in 1929-30, and later by the collapse of the Bank of the United States, with its 59 different affiliates."[19]

Glass was pleased with the way the subcommittee's hearings had gone and with the publicity they received. He thought that his bill had a good chance of enactment. There had been general support by government witnesses for major banking reform legislation. Meanwhile, the Depression was deepening, and bank failures were increasing. In 1928, 491 banks failed; in 1929, 651; thereafter the number skyrocketed to 1,352 in 1930 and to 2,294 in 1931.[20] These dire developments made it more likely that major banking legislation could be enacted.

Glass would have recalled that the Federal Reserve Act had been enacted in 1913 over strong bank opposition because President Wilson had provided leadership. While commercial bankers at the 1931 hearings had opposed most reforms, Glass believed that the hearings would force President Hoover to support his bill or result in enactment of even more comprehensive legislation. Glass may not have anticipated the extent of the problems he would face with President Hoover.

The Hoover Administration

On the surface, President Hoover seemed well-suited to leading the nation in combating the Great Depression. He had been an extremely successful engineer before the First World War, led America's war relief efforts in Europe, and served with distinction in the cabinets of both Presidents Harding and Coolidge.

But Hoover was not cut out for a leadership role in confronting the nation's economic problems. One of Hoover's biographers, Joan Huff Wilson, noted that after the Great Depression began, "his methods remained essentially what they had been throughout the previous decade of prosperity: reliance on persuasion to raise private funds voluntarily, educational conferences, fact-finding commissions, and decentralized voluntary implementation of decisions reached by a centralized administrative source." Two contemporary writers, Marcus Nadler and Jules Bogen, put it more succinctly: "It was a characteristic of the Hoover regime that problems were tackled through the expedient of forming commissions to study them."[21]

Hoover's general passivity was evident in his approach to banking reform. As Susan Kennedy has noted, while Hoover repeatedly recommended possible reforms such as limiting long-term loans by banks, separating banks and their security affiliates, and statewide branching by national banks, "nothing came of any of these proposals during his term in office, and in fact Hoover put them forth only gratuitously. He did not press for any fundamental changes, nor did he endorse others' efforts to secure reform."[22] In today's parlance, Hoover talked the talk, but did not walk the walk. Hoover took no legislative initiatives on banking matters during his entire term in office, 1929 to 1933.

Willis believed that Hoover's passivity was designed to prevent the enactment of banking reform legislation, stating:

> President Hoover ... was inclined, during the campaign of 1932, to refer occasionally to banking reform as a policy or program which had enjoyed his own special approval or recommendation.... A careful scrutiny of his published speeches and addresses, however, fails to disclose any advocacy of new banking legislation, and it was common knowledge in Congress that, at the outset of his administration, it had been the wish of the Treasury Department, presumably with Mr. Hoover's assent, to have matters so arranged that legislation relating to branch banking and to other kindred matters would not make its appearance on the floor.[23]

Instead of working for broad financial reform legislation, Hoover sought enactment of specific "emergency" measures. These included legislation creating the Reconstruction Finance Corporation, which provided loans to state and local governments, banks, railroads, mortgage associations, and other businesses, and the Glass-Steagall Act of 1933, which expanded the collateral Federal Reserve Banks could accept for loans to member banks. Nadler and Bogen alleged that these emergency measures were intended by Hoover and his allies in the administration and banking community "to stall off the day of reckoning" on comprehensive banking reform. Willis later wrote that these delaying tactics worked and "retarded the further consideration of the Glass measure."[24]

It is impossible to determine whether Hoover and his associates intended to block comprehensive banking reform legislation or whether Hoover's passivity and uncertainty simply had this effect. In either case, the outcome was the same: Glass was largely on his own in seeking omnibus banking reform legislation. The president, the Secretary of the Treasury, the Comptroller of the Currency, the Federal Reserve Board, and the general banking community either were opposed to major banking legislation or were standing on the sidelines. "Only the Banking and Currency Committee of the United States Senate concerned itself with the problem of fundamental banking reform, through the investigation launched by its sub-committee headed by Carter Glass."[25]

Glass's Second Bill: Elimination of Bank Security Affiliates

Glass continued to work on his legislation as the Depression deepened. In January 1932, a second version of Glass's bill, S. 3215, was reported out of his subcommittee and went to the full Senate Banking and Currency Committee.[26] Glass believed that the most important provisions were those designed to limit bank lending to finance securities speculation. Other provisions dealt with branching, capital requirements for national banks, and creation of a liquidation corporation for failed banks. Glass believed that strong capital requirements and the prompt payment of liquidation proceeds to depositors were preferable to federal insurance of deposits.[27]

Glass's second bill marked a sea change in his approach to bank security affiliates. Like Glass's first bill, S. 3215 severely restricted direct national bank securities activities, to acting only as brokers upon the orders of customers. But whereas Glass's first bill would have subjected bank securities affiliates to regulation by the Comptroller of the Currency and the Federal Reserve Board, Glass's second bill would eliminate bank securities affiliates altogether. The second bill did this by adopting two provisions similar to those that John Broderick, Superintendent of Banking for the State of New York, had testified that he was recommending to the New York State legislature regarding New York State–chartered banks. First, Section 20 of S. 3215 provided that certificates for stock in a national bank could not simultaneously represent stock in any other corporation. Second, Section 21 provided that an officer of a national bank or a state member bank could not also serve as an officer or employee of a company engaged primarily in the business of purchasing, selling, or negotiating securities. Section 23 additionally required every shareholder of a national bank to file a sworn statement that he was not also a shareholder of any security affiliate of the bank.

It would take something significant to cause Glass to move from proposing to regulate securities affiliates in his first bill to proposing their total elimination in his second. Several months after the introduction of his second bill, in May 1932, Glass wrote to a Virginia banker that he personally had not favored elimination, but that other members of the Senate Banking Committee insisted on this draconian approach: "I may say that it was my opinion, as expressed in committee, that affiliates of national banks might better be continued under searching examination and restrictions of federal authority than disassociated from parent banks at the end of a three or five year period; but the committee thought otherwise and provided for disassociation."

In his 1934 book, Willis offered a similar explanation:

Members of the Committee had received great numbers of letters from citizens of all classes who were outraged by what they considered the injustice to which they had been subjected through the affiliate system and who demanded absolute elimination of it—root and branch— from the national banking and Federal Reserve system. Accordingly, it was determined to set aside the original plan and to substitute that of completely separating parent banks from their affiliate enterprises.[28]

Glass's and Willis's after-the-fact explanations do not ring true. Glass was the last person to be moved by his colleagues if he thought they were wrong. During the time that he was developing his second bill, Glass wrote several letters that demonstrated that he personally had moved from being open to regulation of security affiliates to supporting their elimination. On December 4, 1931, Winthrop A. Mandell wrote to Glass, "no bank should have an affiliate in the security business." The next day Glass replied, "You may be assured that I agree with everything you say about bank affiliates and I hope to impress those views on my sub-committee and upon Congress."

On December 23, 1931, Glass wrote to E. A. Purdy, "I am writing now to say that the subcommittee on Banking and Currency of which I am chairman seriously contemplates the abolition of bank affiliates. My own information is that this should be done."[29] Glass certainly sounded more like someone who was leading the charge for elimination, rather than a follower.

It appears from the evidence that Glass moved from being open to regulation to favoring elimination not because of pressure from other senators and voters, but because of his growing belief that regulation was unlikely to work. As discussed above, on the second day of the hearings, Glass stated that he was amenable to a regulatory approach to security affiliates if it was "possible to control them in some way"; otherwise, he would be "agreeable to prohibiting them."[30] It appears that Glass concluded from the hearings that control of security affiliates via regulation was highly unlikelybecause of a number of factors.

First, security affiliates posed a host of complex problems. At the start, Glass and Willis believed that security affiliates only raised an example of unsound lending by banks since banks tended to make large loans to their security affiliates. It would have been fairly easy to restrict the amount of loans a bank could make to its security affiliate. Indeed, in March 1930, Willis sent Glass legislative language to do this.[31] However, as Glass and Willis learned more about bank security affiliates, it became clear that there were numerous other types of problems, which were enumerated in the subcommittee's report.

Second, there was no existing regulatory body with the ability to adequately regulate bank security affiliates. Glass's first bill provided that the regulators of security affiliates were to be the Comptroller of the Currency in the case of affiliates of national banks and the Federal Reserve Board in the case of affiliates of state-chartered banks that were members of the Federal Reserve System. However, these banking agencies had no experience in regulating nonbank entities such as security affiliates. Moreover, neither banking agency had a particularly good track record in regulating *banks*. As early as 1923, Glass concluded that the office of the Comptroller of the Currency was so ineffective that it should be abolished, a view that he still held in the 1930s.[32]

The Federal Reserve Board had its own regulatory problems. In the late 1920s, the Fed had largely ignored Glass's pleas to use its general regulatory authority to curb bank loans for securities speculation. On April 6, 1931, Glass wrote: "It is my view that the banks openly defied the explicit requirements of the law and that the Board submissively acquiesced in the flaunting of its powers and authority.... had the Board at Washington promptly dismissed Mitchell [of First National City Bank and a member of the New York Fed] when he defied its authority and brazenly announced his purpose to violate the law [the Fed's admonition against security loans], it is my judgment that the riot of speculation in New York would have abruptly been abated."[33]

Third, the Fed itself shared Glass's concerns about the lack of efficacy of a regulatory approach. At the subcommittee's hearings before Glass moved to separation, the Fed testified that it preferred separation but supported regulation because it was difficult to "unscramble" existing relationships. This was hardly a ringing endorsement of the regulatory approach. Statements by Fed officials after Glass moved to separation also indicate that the Fed favored separation. At the full committee hearings, the Fed presented a draft provision providing for separation, although the Fed's testimony said that this was not a recommendation. Later, on September 29, 1932, Federal Reserve Board member Charles Hamlin wrote to Glass that the practice of big banks' requiring small correspondent banks to invest in securities distributed by the big banks' security affiliates "certainly would seem to justify the clause in your bill requiring member banks to divorce themselves from their affiliates."[34]

Fourth, the Bank of the United States failed just before the Glass subcommittee began its hearings. There was widespread belief that the bank's failure was because of its fifty-nine affiliates. Rightly or wrongly, many people believed that this cast grave suspicions on bank *security affiliates*. The report of the Glass subcommittee ended by noting the impact of the failure on public opinion regarding security affiliates.

On July 13, 1931, the *New York Times* reported that leading bankers predicted, correctly, that the failure of the Bank of the United States would give impetus to measures requiring separation of banks and their security affiliates, "In the opinion of bankers, the collapse of this institution was due entirely to its many investment affiliates and not to the workings of the bank itself. It is to be expected, leading bankers hold, that some move to divorce all banks from their investment affiliates may get under way next Winter."[35]

Finally, the failure of the Bank of the United States led New York State Superintendent Broderick to introduce state legislation mandating separation of New York State–chartered banks and their security affiliates. Separation was no longer a theoretical idea, but now was incorporated in proposed statutory language in the most important financial state in the nation.

Glass was a practical politician, not an ideologue. The evidence indicates that initially Glass was open to a regulatory approach, but that a number of factors (growing awareness of the complex problems posed by security affiliates, the absence of a capable regulator, the Fed's doubts about the efficacy of regulation, the failure of the Bank of the United States, and Broderick's actions in New York State) caused Glass to move from being open to regulation to favoring separation.

Raymond Moley, an adviser to President Roosevelt, later asserted that "the divorcement of commercial banks from their security affiliates ... had ... been a major purpose of Glass from the beginning."[36]

While there is no evidence to support Moley's claim, Glass undoubtedly remembered that in 1913, the Pujo subcommittee had recommended the elimination of security affiliates and that Brandeis had echoed this view in his book *Other People's Money*. Most likely, Glass began the hearings with a bias in favor of separation but was open to arguments supporting regulation. Hearing none, it would have been easy for Glass to move in favor of separation.

Glass was careful not to get too far in front of popular opinion on a controversial issue and thereby jeopardize the chances for any major banking reform legislation. Letters from voters and entreaties of other senators calling for separation gave Glass the cover he needed to openly move in that direction. It is easy to understand why Glass did not want to spell out the real reason for his movement to separation ("Regulation of bank security affiliates by the Comptroller of the Currency and the Federal Reserve Board is unlikely to work, as the Board itself admits") since this would embarrass the Board and the Comptroller and could rattle an already frightened public. It was easier for Glass to say, "other Senators made me do it."

9. Glass Admonishes the Stock Market. Copyright 1932. Used with permission from *The Baltimore Sun*.

Similarly, the Board probably did not want to admit publicly that it and the Comptroller could not handle the regulatory job and did not want to get into a fight with the Comptroller and the banking industry, both of whom opposed separation. So, the Board was quite happy with Glass's explanation that pressure from other senators on his subcommittee caused him to move from regulation to separation.

Glass's revised bill elicited very different reactions. On the one hand, Senator Norbeck, the Republican chairman of the Banking and Currency Committee, called Glass's bill "the most important piece of banking legislation before the committee for ten years," and predicted little or no controversy in the committee. On the other hand, as Nadler and Bogen noted, "the introduction of the Glass Bill was the signal for one of the most violent and vociferous attacks delivered against any measure brought before Congress witnessed in years. Bankers' associations, individual financiers and chambers of commerce joined in condemning it as a vicious bill and an insuperable bar to economic recovery.... Opposition was particularly strong from ... many leading New York bankers who sought to save their security affiliates."[37]

Glass responded to these critics by delivering a blistering speech on the floor of the Senate: "Here are people who confessedly have not read the provisions of the bill, and who do not understand the measure, wiring all over the country suggesting that the banking associations of the respective States wire to their senators in opposition to a bill the precise meaning of which they do not yet comprehend." He went on to point out that this was a repetition of bankers' behavior eighteen years before when they had opposed the Federal Reserve Act.[38]

Glass's Third and Fourth Bills: The Push for Separation

The full Senate Banking Committee held hearings in March 1932 on a newly revised third version of Glass's bill, S. 4115.[39] A series of bank witnesses testified in strong opposition to the provisions that would separate banks and their security affiliates. Eugene Meyer, a Governor of the Federal Reserve Board, presented a letter from the Board on the entire bill. While the letter did not make an explicit recommendation that banks and their security affiliates be separated, it seemed to indicate that the board *supported* this approach, by stating, "the board realizes that many evils have developed through the operation of affiliates connected with member banks, particularly affiliates dealing in securities. The attached memorandum contains a draft of a provision for the separation of affiliates after a lapse of three years." However, in his testimony, Meyer stated that the board was not making a definite recommendation but was simply submitting the provision for consideration by the Senate committee. After the hearings, Glass wrote to Meyer to complain that the board had been asked to present its "authoritative suggestions" and that the committee did not need "unauthorized advice."[40]

Next, Glass revised his bill once again, as S. 4412, which was reported to the full Senate in April.[41] This fourth bill contained a new section, Section 19, as mentioned by Fed Governor Meyer: "After five years from the date of enactment of this Act, no member bank shall be affiliated in any manner ... with any corporation, association, business trust, or other similar organization engaged principally in the issue, flotation, underwriting, public sale, or distribution at wholesale or retail or through syndicate participation of stocks, bonds, debentures, notes, or other securities." The committee report that accompanied S. 4412 sharply criticized bank security affiliates, stressing the use of bank resources to fund the speculative activities of affiliates:

There seems to be no doubt anywhere that a large factor in the overdevelopment of security loans, and in the dangerous use of the resources of bank depositors for the purpose of making speculative profits and incurring

10. "Glass Criticizes Republicans During the 1932 Campaign."
Copyright 1932. Used with permission from *The Baltimore Sun*.

the danger of hazardous losses, has been furnished by perversions of the national and State banking laws, and that, as a result, machinery has been created which tends toward danger in several directions. (a) The greatest of such dangers in seen in the growth of "bank affiliates" which devote themselves in many cases to perilous underwriting operations, stock speculation, and maintaining a market for the banks' own stock often largely with the resources of the parent bank. This situation was never contemplated by the national banking act, and it would, therefore, appear that the affiliate system calls for the establishment of some legislative provisions designed to deal with the situation.[42]

During the debate on the bill on the Senate floor in May 1932, Glass stated that the "committee ascertained in a more or less definite way—we think quite a definite way—that one of the greatest contributions to the unprecedented disaster which has caused this almost incurable depression was made by these bank affiliates."[43]

Glass also produced an important historical document. In a speech on the Senate floor in May 1932, he presented a 1911 opinion by Solicitor General Lehmann, concurred in by Attorney General Wickersham, holding that the security affiliate of First National City Bank was an "usurpation of Federal authority and in violation of Federal law." Glass had a carbon copy of the original opinion, which was missing. The Taft Administration had not taken any legal action to implement the opinion's findings. It appeared that the entire affiliate system always had been illegal but had been protected by a cover-up as well as lax, or corrupt, administration. Therefore, legislation requiring separation was justified.[44]

Glass hoped his bill could be brought to the Senate floor in June. However, the Republican leadership held the bill over until the December session.

The Election of Franklin Roosevelt

Glass worked for the nomination of Newton D. Baker as the Democratic presidential candidate in 1932.[45] However, after the Democratic convention nominated Franklin Delano Roosevelt, Glass worked for Roosevelt's election.

Glass wrote the portion of the Democrats' platform that called for "the severance of affiliated security companies from and the divorce of the investment banking business from commercial banks and further restrictions of Federal reserve banks in permitting the use of Federal reserve facilities for speculative purposes."[46] In a major campaign address in Columbus, Ohio, FDR echoed Glass's views regarding both bank lending for speculative purposes and bank security affiliates:

> Fifth—We have witnessed not only the unrestricted use of bank deposits in speculation to the detriment of local credit, but we are also aware that this speculation was encouraged by the Government itself. I propose that such speculation be discouraged and prevented. Sixth—Investment banking is a legitimate business. Commercial banking is a wholly separate and distinct business. Their consolidation and mingling are contrary to public policy. I propose their separation. Seventh—Prior to the Panic of 1929 the funds of the Federal Reserve System were used practically without check for many speculative enterprises. I propose the restrictions of Federal Reserve Banks in accordance with the original plans and early practices of the Federal Reserve System under Woodrow Wilson.[47]

Glass delivered a major radio address supporting FDR's election, in which he sharply criticized the Hoover Administration's record on financial matters, including permitting bank security activities:

With insatiable avarice, great banking institutions in the United States, through their lawless affiliates with their high-pressure salesmanship, brought over and unloaded on the investing public of America billions of dollars of foreign securities, now practically worthless.*** Undeniably, they filled the portfolios of interior banks, sometimes by coercion, with this immobile junk, so that when the crash came these banks were in a state of paralysis, utterly unable to respond to the legitimate requirements of their respective communities.*** With Mr. Andrew W. Mellon as Chairman of the [Federal Reserve] Board and the predominant figure, in a single six-month period in 1929 ten of the largest banks in New York alone were given access to seven hundred and fifty millions of dollars of Federal Reserve credits under the fifteen-day provision of the [Federal Reserve] Act. Plainly interpreted, this means that a large, if not a greater, part of this sum, was being loaned to brokers for stock-gambling purposes.[48]

Glass also criticized the various "emergency" measures enacted at President Hoover's urging and contrasted them with the approach the Democrats would take: "We shall not rely upon transient devices and mere temporary remedies for serious situations; but, holding fast to sound Jeffersonian principles and applying tested orthodox processes, we shall hope to rescue the government and the country from the unendurable confusion and distress into which the Republican maladministration has thrust us."[49]

The *Washington Herald* called Glass's address "the outstanding speech of the campaign, in either party." A columnist in the *Washington Evening Star* wrote: "It was one of the radio events of the epoch." Even the chairman of Chase National Bank wrote Glass to say it was "the best speech during the campaign." Roosevelt sent a telegram to

Glass setting forth his "heartiest congratulations and sincere appreciation for your wonderful speech last night. I listened to all of it and was thrilled and inspired."[50]

Following Roosevelt's landslide election victory, Glass turned to seeking Congressional approval of his bill in the lame-duck session preceding FDR's inauguration in March 1933. Chances looked good. Professor Edwin Perkins has observed that "positive Congressional action during the 1932–1933 winter session seemed like a real possibility after the President-elect, without commenting specifically on any of its actual provisions, gave the legislation his general endorsement."[51]

Glass began his efforts in the Senate. He pushed for quick passage of his bill by announcing for the first time that the president-elect supported it. He also made a number of concessions designed to improve the bill's chances, including lengthening the period national banks would be allowed for divorcing their security affiliates and permitting national banks to underwrite state and municipal general obligation bonds: "Although Glass wanted national banks to be completely removed from any investment banking business other than that conducted for their trust accounts or own funds, he agreed to the amendment in the belief that state governments would encourage their congressmen to support the measure now that they were assured of an orderly market for their bonds."[52]

Glass's biggest stumbling block was a filibuster by Senator Huey Long of Louisiana that lasted more than a week. Long vehemently opposed the bill's branching provisions, which he viewed as a threat to unit banks, which were particularly common in his state. The Senate leaders threatened to end Long's filibuster by invoking cloture, and Glass modified the branching provisions. Long relented, and at long last, on January 25, 1933, the Senate passed Glass's bill by an overwhelming vote of 54 to 9.

The bill was sent to the House of Representatives. Glass asked President-elect Roosevelt to tell House Democrats to vote for passage.

Although Roosevelt previously had supported the bill in the Senate, he indicated that he could not back it in the House in its present form. Susan Kennedy wrote: "Roosevelt believed the Glass proposals did not go far enough; he wanted protection of investors against fictitious or bad securities, segregation of savings from commercial deposits, revision of the liquidating corporation clause to permit immediate reopening of failed banks, and branch banking limited to no more than a countywide basis."[53] It also is likely that Roosevelt did not want banking reform legislaton enacted until he became president, so that he could share in the credit.

As the lame-duck session of Congress ended in early 1933, Glass had much to be proud of. In 1930, he had launched the most exhaustive look into American banking since the National Monetary Commission in 1908. Over the course of three years, he had developed a comprehensive banking reform bill that addressed key areas, such as bank lending to securities firms, bank security affiliates, branching, and liquidation procedures for failed banks. Glass had adjusted and compromised as needed. He had introduced successive versions of his bill while maintaining the core elements of reform. Meanwhile, he had resisted including a deposit insurance program, which he viewed as most unwise. He had stood up to and defeated the organized commercial banking community. He had survived the passivity, if not the hostility, of the Hoover Administration. He helped write the banking portion of the Democrats' 1932 platform. He had guided his bill through the Senate, where it received overwhelming support. Glass's hard work, tenacity, and "pluck" had paid off once again.

Glass was near total victory. His one remaining hurdle was the role of the new president. FDR had supported Glass's bill in the Senate during the lame-duck session, but he had declined to do so in the House of Representatives. Glass likely wondered how his bill could make it through the new Congress without President Roosevelt's support.

6
ENACTMENT OF
THE GLASS-STEAGALL ACT

There is no luck. Luck is the residue of design.

—Branch Rickey

When Franklin Roosevelt became president in early 1933, it was unclear how committed he would be to Glass's banking reform bill. Glass used three developments he personally opposed—the national bank holiday, increased public demand for deposit insurance, and the Pecora hearings on stock market abuses—to obtain enactment of his bill, in the form of the Glass-Steagall Act. The absence of direct support from the president did not prevent Glass's success.

President Franklin Roosevelt Assumes Office

In March 1933, a new president, Franklin Delano Roosevelt, the first Democratic president since Woodrow Wilson, was inaugurated. A new Congress, with both houses firmly controlled by the Democrats, began its sessions. It was unclear how committed President Roosevelt would be to enactment of Glass's banking reform bill in the new congress. During the previous lame-duck session, he had supported Glass's bill in the Senate, where it passed, but had declined to do so in the House of Representatives, where it died.

In early 1933, three major developments occurred—the March

bank holiday, increased public demand for federal deposit insurance, and new congressional hearings on stock market practices. Although Glass opposed all three developments, he used them to help obtain enactment of his banking reform bill. Against this background, the absence of help from FDR did not prove to be a serious detriment to the enactment of Glass's bill.

The March 1933 Bank Holiday

Near the end of the 1932 presidential campaign, a unique event took place. For the first time in American history, because of depositor runs, one state, Utah, temporarily permitted *all* banks within its borders to suspend operations. The event received little notice since it was because of an unusual set of facts (bad livestock loans by one group of banks) and involved a very small state.

However, the bank "holiday" in Utah foreshadowed a fresh wave of depositor runs and bank suspensions across the nation. These disruptions occurred during the four-month interregnum between the election of Franklin Roosevelt in November 1932 and his inauguration in March 1933, a continuation of a terrible downturn in the American economy. Susan Kennedy has written: "The United States suffered radical drops in employment from the latter part of October through early March. Fifteen million persons had no jobs; many others were working at reduced wages. At least three million crowded the relief roles; and in countless places welfare facilities had broken down entirely.... Prices of farm products fell off ruinously, as did the commodities and stock markets.... in November ... [Bank] failures exceeded openings by $30.8 million; losses doubled in December and quadrupled in January."[1]

In the face of these cascading disasters, President Hoover found new grounds for passivity during his final months in office. Kennedy wrote: "Hoover knew that the voters had rejected him and felt that all energy now belonged to his more popular successor; therefore, he never considered vigorous action on his own to counteract the economic slide."[2] Hoover maintained that he would only act if he had the public support of the president-elect. Roosevelt refused to offer that backing, on the grounds that only the president, and not the president-elect, had authority to act.

In response to depositor runs, Louisiana joined Nevada in announcing a bank holiday in February 1932. Later that month, Michigan became the first large industrial state to declare a bank holiday. Marcus Nadler and Jules Bogen wrote, "The closing of the Michigan banks marked the beginning of the final crash. From then on the drama of the collapse rose rapidly to the climax and engulfed state after state. The grand finale was on. Michigan was the last straw that broke the camel's back and set in motion a maddened rush on the part of the depositors for their money."[3] Citing the need to prevent withdrawals in reaction to Michigan's suspension, Indiana, Maryland, Arkansas, and Ohio announced bank holidays. Other states were heading toward suspensions. Several of President Hoover's advisers urged him to take emergency action under the World War I Trading-with-the-Enemy Act and declare a *nationwide* bank holiday. But, once again, Hoover hesitated. His administration ended without taking action.

When Roosevelt was sworn in as president on Saturday, March 4, 1933, the banks in the major financial centers were closed. By that afternoon, all forty-eight states had declared bank holidays. In his inaugural address, Roosevelt castigated the bankers as "money-changers" who "have fled from their high seats in the temple of our civilization." He called for major banking reform legislation: "There must be a strict supervision of all banking and credits and investments; there must be an end to speculation with other people's money." He explicitly rejected the passive approach followed by his predecessor: "This Nation asks for action, and action now." He expressed the hope that "the normal balance of executive and legislative authority" would prove sufficient to meet the crisis. However, he went on to declare that if they proved inadequate, "I shall ask the Congress for the one remaining instrument to meet the crisis—broad Executive power to wage a war against the emergency, as great as the power that would be given to me if we were in fact invaded by a foreign foe."[4]

Roosevelt followed these words with immediate action. On Monday, March 6, using a draft prepared for President Hoover, he issued a proclamation under the authority of the Trading-with-the-Enemy Act closing *all* banks in the country for four days. Glass had told the new president, as he previously had told President Hoover, that he had no constitutional authority to close state-chartered banks that were not members of the Federal Reserve System. Glass also pointed out that the Trading-with-the-Enemy Act had expired. Glass wrote privately, "I think the President of the United States had no more valid authority to close or to open a bank in the United States than had my stable boy."[5] But Glass said nothing in public.

President Roosevelt called Congress into special session on March 9 to vote on emergency banking legislation. The emergency bill was drafted by the Roosevelt Administration, based on a proposal that had been prepared by Hoover's Secretary of the Treasury Ogden Mills. The bill approved the nationwide bank holiday and set forth a basis for licensing sound banks to reopen. The bill reflected changes that were urged by Glass, notably the exclusion of state banks that were not members of the Federal Reserve System from the licensing provisions.

The bill passed the House of Representatives just one hour after Congress convened. That afternoon it went immediately to the Senate, where Glass, later described by Anthony Badger as "possibly the only member of the Congress who understood the technicalities of the legislation," guided the bill through.[6] Senator Huey Long, a Democrat from Louisiana, proposed an amendment to give the president authority to bring all state-chartered banks into the Federal Reserve System and thus cause them to be covered by the licensing process. Glass ended the debate when he stated, "There are provisions in the bill to which in ordinary times I would not dream of subscribing, but we have a situation that invites the patriotic cooperation and aid of every man who has any regard for his country and for its business interest. I appeal to you, Senators, not to load it down with amendments." As Glass and Long left the Senate floor, they almost got into a fist-fight.[7] That evening, the Senate passed the bill by a vote of 73 to 7, and President Roosevelt signed the bill into law as the Emergency Banking Act of 1933.

The licensing process set forth in the Emergency Banking Act proved to be a great success. Most banks were allowed to resume business in a short period of time. Under Roosevelt's decisive leadership (with Glass's help in the Senate), the crisis had been met.

The 1933 banking crisis, including the bank holiday, produced a broad public consensus that major banking reform legislation was needed to ensure that similar crises would not occur in the future. The events surrounding the bank holiday gave a huge impetus to Glass's bill. Glass had been wise not to publicly voice his belief that FDR's proclamation of the bank holiday had been illegal and unconstitutional.

Increased Public Demand for Federal Deposit Insurance

Government insurance of bank deposits has a long history in the United States.[8] In 1829, New York became the first state to enact legislation establishing a state insurance fund, to which all banks seeking charter renewal were required contributors. Other states, including Vermont, Michigan, Indiana, and Ohio, followed. These early state insurance schemes generally worked well. However, they ceased operations in the mid-nineteenth century. Public interest in government insurance of bank deposits returned after the Civil War. Between 1886 and the turn of the century, eighteen bills providing for *federal* insurance of deposits were introduced in Congress, but none were enacted. The Panic of 1907 led eight states, Oklahoma, Kansas, Nebraska, Texas, Mississippi, South Dakota, North Dakota, and Washington, to enact legislation guaranteeing deposits in state-chartered banks. These state schemes initially worked well. However, the agricultural depression of the 1920s and the large number of bank failures in the late 1920s and early 1930s ended their effectiveness. Meanwhile, more and more bills were introduced in Congress providing for federal deposit insurance. Between 1886 and 1933, some 150 separate proposals were offered.

There were three main reasons why proponents wanted government insurance of bank deposits. First and most obviously, they wanted to protect depositors, particularly small depositors. Second, as Carter Golombe noted, supporters of deposit insurance sought "to restore to the community, as quickly as possible, circulating medium destroyed or made unavailable as a consequence of bank failures. In this view, bank-obligation insurance has a monetary function."[9]

Even many of those who wanted insurance in order to protect depositors still stressed the monetary argument. For example, in 1932, Senator Robert L. Owen testified: "The first observation I wish to make is that to provide the people of the United States with an absolutely safe place and a convenient place to put their savings and their deposits is essential to the stability of banking, bank deposits and loans, the checks which function as money, and business conditions in every line.... It is a far greater matter than the very important end of protecting the individual depositor or the bank from loss."[10]

The third rationale for deposit insurance related to the argument over banking structure—the argument between those who favored thousands of individual one-office banks and those who favored fewer and larger banks with numerous branches. Proponents of small unit banks saw government insurance of deposits as a way to "save small banks" from competition from outsiders. Opponents of deposit insurance thought it would save small banks that deserved to fail and prevent the natural development of sounder competitive branching.

The leader of the effort in Congress for federal deposit insurance was the powerful chairman of the House Committee on Banking and Currency, Democratic Representative Henry A. Steagall of Alabama. In April 1932, while Hoover was still in office, Steagall introduced a deposit insurance bill that passed the House after just four hours of debate. Glass refused to sponsor a similar bill in the Senate, and the legislation died. The issue was bound to come up again when the new congress convened.

Most experts on banking in that era opposed government insurance of deposits. Large banks believed that it would require large well-run banks to pay insurance premiums to subsidize small weak institutions and thereby encourage "wild-cat management." President Roosevelt was opposed to deposit insurance. "Like the bankers," Michael Perino pointed out, "Roosevelt saw the proposal as requiring stronger banks to subsidize weaker ones, thereby creating disincentives for prudent management. Throughout the debate, Roosevelt continually threatened to veto any bill that contained an insurance provision."[11] Glass felt the same way. Alfred Cash Koeniger wrote: "Glass had long opposed deposit insurance. If funded by assessments against the banks, he thought, it forced sound institutions to pay for others' mismanagement. He feared strong banks would leave the reserve system before subsidizing their less secure competitors, and in any case it was unfair to penalize the strong and virtuous in order to put them on equal footing with the weak and irresponsible."[12]

Deposit insurance presented Glass with a doubtful political advantage. Inclusion of deposit insurance in Glass's bill would help obtain congressional enactment. On the other hand, if deposit insurance was added to the bill, there was the danger that President Roosevelt would veto it. It is impossible to overstate how popular federal deposit insurance was with the public, and with the owners of small town banks and their political allies. In April 1932, Chairman

Steagall had warned House Speaker John Nance Garner, "You know, this fellow Hoover is going to wake up one day and come in here with a message recommending guarantee of bank deposits, and as sure as he does, he'll be re-elected."[13] Hoover missed this opportunity. Glass had a chance to add deposit insurance to his bill in order to obtain its enactment.

The Pecora Hearings on Stock Exchange Practices

After the 1929 stock market crash, President Hoover tried to persuade the New York Stock Exchange to improve its regulation of questionable speculative practices such as short sales and bear raids. Hoover's calls for stronger self-regulation by the exchange fell on deaf ears. Frustrated by the lack of response, Hoover threatened a congressional investigation and legislation providing for federal regulation of stock exchanges. The NYSE remained unresponsive. Finally, in February 1932, Hoover asked the Senate Banking and Currency Committee to conduct an investigation into stock exchange practices.

Glass opposed the stock exchange hearings since he feared that they might delay consideration of his banking reform bill until after the November elections. However, Glass was unable to prevent the hearings because of President Hoover's pressure on Republican members of the committee to hold hearings. Hearings were held from April through June. They focused almost exclusively on manipulative practices. But nothing happened with respect to new legislation. The hearings resumed in January 1933 with only five or six weeks remaining in the lame-duck congressional session. In that short time, the committee had to examine witnesses, sift through the evidence, and prepare a report with recommendations to Congress.

The chairman of the Committee, Senator Peter Norbeck, a Republican from South Dakota, retained a new counsel for the subcommittee, Ferdinand Pecora, an attorney in New York City who had served as chief assistant district attorney for New York County.

The appointment proved serendipitous. Pecora's first step was to rec-ommend that Norbeck broaden the hearings beyond manipulative practices and launch an investigation into high-pressure sales of new issues of securities during the 1920s. Norbeck was bowled over by Pecora's suggestion, and asked, "Under this language [of the resolu-tion authorizing the hearings] would it have been possible for my committee to inquire into the ways by which the people through-out my state were high-pressured into buying millions and millions and millions of dollars worth of securities that were sour?" Pecora assured him that this indeed was the case. Norbeck then authorized the investigation into sales practices.[14]

Pecora's main target was the giant New York City commercial bank, National City Bank, and its security affiliate, National City Company, which by the late 1920s had become the largest securities firm in the nation. Both the bank and the securities affiliate were headed by Charles E. Mitchell, whom Glass previously had iden-tified as the individual most responsible for the 1929 stock market crash.

Although Pecora had very limited time in which to prepare, he did an outstanding job during hearings in February and March 1932. He attacked the entire commercial bank–security affiliate structure. He presented Solicitor General Frederick Lehmann's 1911 opinion that it was a violation of federal law for a national bank to have a security affiliate. As discussed in Chapter 5, Glass previously had released a copy of the opinion. Glass had not, however, revealed the identities of the bank and the affiliate. Pecora named names—the bank was National City Bank, and the security affiliate was National City Com-pany. With Mitchell as a witness, Pecora demonstrated that the bank had "completely controlled the affiliate."[15] He showed that the affili-ate was one vast machine for mass-marketing securities to investors throughout the nation. Susan Kennedy observed: "Mitchell built up a finely articulated network comprising 11,386 miles of private wires, sixty-nine district offices in fifty-eight cities, sales representatives in the bank's twenty-six branches, and smaller dealers including investment departments of other banks."[16] Many of these securities became worthless.

Most telling to the public were revelations about a host of transactions where the security affiliate ripped off small investors to benefit National City Bank, or even worse, to benefit Mitchell personally. "In truth," Pecora's biographer Michael Perino wrote, "the picture Pecora painted on that first day of testimony was of a corporation run with only a single purpose in mind—to maximize the financial return of its officers, especially its chairman. Nothing else seemed to matter. Not the shareholders, who were kept in the dark about how much the officers were raking in; not the customers, who trusted the institution to provide them with sound financial advice; and certainly not the federal government, whose tax bills could be easily evaded with a couple of ledger entries."[17] The hearings led Mitchell to resign in disgrace from the bank and the affiliate in February 1933.

As previously mentioned, Glass had opposed holding the stock exchange hearings. Moreover, he complained that Pecora "employed argumentative, courtroom-like tactics in his interrogation, and that the hearings had degenerated into a sensational vendetta against the financial community."[18] Michael Perino has speculated that "Glass must have been a little chagrined about the success Pecora was having. He knew far more about the banking system than Pecora ever would, and most of the same critique of securities affiliates had been made in Glass's earlier hearings."[19] However, Pecora was getting headlines because his hearings were held in the midst of the banking crisis and because he was not focusing on financial theory, but on an actual bank, an actual security affiliate, and an actual banker villain.

While Glass may have been envious of Pecora's success, he used the Pecora hearings to argue for enactment of his banking reform bill, stating, "These disclosures ... prove conclusively the truth of what I said on the Senate floor four years ago—at the height of the boom—namely, that the Federal Reserve System was being used to

11. Franklin Roosevelt signs the Glass-Steagall banking reform act. June 16, 1933. Credit: Everett Collection Historical / Alamy Stock Photo.

aid the speculators rather than those for whom it was created."[20]

Enactment of the Glass-Steagall Act

After passage of the Emergency Banking Act in early March 1933, the Roosevelt Administration made enactment of permanent banking reform legislation a priority. Glass reintroduced his omnibus banking bill. The Senate Banking Committee appointed a subcommittee chaired by Glass to consider the bill. Representative Steagall introduced a similar bill in the House. Discussions began among representatives of the Roosevelt White House, the Treasury Department, the Federal Reserve Board, Senator Glass, Representative Steagall, and other members of Congress.

Most issues were resolved relatively easily, including chain and group banking, minimum capital for new banks, a prohibition of payment of interest on checking accounts, and regulators' ability to remove unfit bank directors and officers.

For many years, Glass's foremost concern had been bank lending to brokers to finance speculation, rather than banks lending to finance commerce. Glass had expressed his concern as Secretary of the Treasury in the Wilson Administration and as a senator during the 1920s, but these efforts had been met with inaction by bank regulators. Given this history, it is not surprising that Glass's bill contained provisions designed to curb banks' extension of credit for securities speculation. Section 3 required Federal Reserve Banks to stay informed about the volume of member bank loans and investments to determine whether undue use was being made of bank credit for stock market speculation. Section 7 empowered the Federal Reserve Board to limit the percentage of bank capital represented by loans collateralized by securities, and it authorized the Fed to order a member bank not to increase its loans for securities activities. The *New York Times* reported: "As to the proposed curbs on use of Federal Reserve funds for speculative purposes, Senator Glass has been fighting for this point for years, and has by this time rallied nearly every member of Congress behind him."[21]

One of the most hotly contested issues in the debate over banking legislation had been Glass's proposal to separate banks and their security affiliates. As discussed in Chapter 5, Glass initially viewed banks' loans to their security affiliates as simply an example of bank lending for securities speculation rather than for commercial purposes. Glass's concern over security affiliates eventually went broader. For example, in early 1933, he declared that:

> I am objecting to affiliates altogether. I am objecting to
> a national banking institution setting up a back-door
> arrangement by which it may engage in a business which

the national bank act denies it the privilege of doing. If investment banking is a profitable business, who does not know that such business will be set up as a separate institution, not using the money and prestige and facilities of a national bank and its deposits to engage in investment activities? I want to make it impossible hereafter to have the portfolios of commercial banks filled with useless speculative securities, so that when stringency comes upon the country these banks may not respond to the requirements of commerce.[22]

As we have seen, in 1931 many conservatives and the commercial banking community in New York City had denounced Glass's proposal to separate banks and their security affiliates. The bank holiday and the Pecora hearings changed everything. Susan Kennedy stated: "The sensational manner of these hearings, as well as their timing, on the eve of the national moratorium, inflamed public resentment. Outrage centered upon the security affiliates, since by 1930 they were sponsoring 54.4 percent of all new securities issues."[23] Academic opinion shifted from opposing Glass's reform efforts to supporting them. As discussed in Chapter 4, in 1929 a Princeton professor had written a book ridiculing Glass's views. After the bank holiday and the Pecora hearings, another Princeton professor, James Gerald Smith, wrote a chapter in a new book excoriating bank security affiliates and calling for legislation that would abolish them.[24]

Moreover, many commercial bankers moved from opposing separation to supporting it. On March 7, 1933, National City Bank announced that it was liquidating its security affiliate. The next day, Winthrop W. Aldrich, chairman of Chase Manhattan Bank, announced that the bank would separate from its security affiliate, Chase Securities Company, "I heartily commend the action of National City Bank in taking steps to divorce its security affiliate.... It is impossible to consider the events which took place during the past ten years without being forced to the conclusion that intimate connection between commercial banking and investment banking almost inevitably leads to abuses."[25] Aldrich not only called for commercial banks to eliminate their security affiliates; he also recommended legislation that would force investment banking firms like J. P. Morgan and Co. to cease accepting deposits.

Glass included in his final bill a series of provisions aimed at separating commercial banking and investment banking:

> **Banks.** Section 16 provided that a national bank's dealing in securities was limited to acting as a broker for customers—"purchasing and selling such securities without recourse, solely upon the order, and for the account of, customers," and that a national bank could not underwrite securities. There was an exception for U.S. government and state securities. Section 5(c) extended these restrictions to state-chartered banks that were members of the Federal Reserve System.
>
> **Security Affiliates.** Section 20 prohibited a bank that was a member of the Federal Reserve System from being affiliated with any company "engaged principally" in "the issue, flotation, underwriting, public sale, or distribution" of securities.
>
> **Securities Firms.** Section 21 prohibited securities firms from taking deposits.
>
> **Personnel.** Section 32 provided that an officer or director of a member bank cannot be an officer or director of a company "primarily engaged" in the business of purchasing or selling securities.

Each provision can be traced to specific events during Glass's three-year development of banking reform legislation. The restrictions on securities activities conducted directly by banks (Section 16) appeared in Glass's original bill, S. 4723. Personnel restrictions between banks and security affiliates (Section 32) were mentioned in Broderick's testimony concerning recommendations he was making to the New York legislature and were set forth in Glass's second bill, S. 3215. The separation of banks and security affiliates (Section 20) was discussed in the testimony of Federal Reserve Board Governor Eugene Meyer and was provided for in Glass's fourth bill, S. 4412. The prohibition against investment banking firms accepting deposits was mentioned by Broderick, urged by Winthrop W. Aldrich of Chase Manhattan Bank, and set forth in Glass's last bill, S. 1631.

Why had Glass offered these provisions in a series of bills, rather that all at once? It is easy to say that commercial banks should be prohibited from engaging, directly and indirectly, in securities activities. It is far more difficult to devise legislative language implementing this policy, particularly the separation of commercial banks and their security affiliates. As Willis later observed, "Separation ... was found to be a rather difficult matter.... The affiliates had always been perfectly legal, regularly established enterprises, operating under state laws. Congress then could only attack them by prescribing the relationships which might or might not exist between corporations (banks) under its jurisdiction and the state corporations (affiliates)."[26]

There was no comprehensive model at the federal or state level that Glass could copy. Witnesses at a series of hearings, including the New York Superintendent of Banking, Federal Reserve Board Governor Meyer, and the chairman of Chase Manhattan Bank, offered various suggestions for implementing separation. Glass adopted these suggestions, as they were offered, in his successive bills. Glass included a complete package in his final bill.

Only one major issue—federal insurance of bank deposits—remained. But that issue threatened to derail enactment of Glass's entire reform bill. Deposit insurance was extremely popular among voters and in Congress, where its champion was Representative Steagall, chairman of the House Banking Committee. The popularity of deposit insurance is demonstrated by the fact that Steagall introduced his deposit insurance bill on April 14, 1933, it was reported out by the House Banking Committee on April 19, and it passed the House on May 25 after only four hours of debate.

Glass had refused to sponsor a similar measure in the Senate. Roosevelt repeatedly indicated that he would veto any bill that provided for deposit insurance. Just before his inauguration, FDR told Vice President-elect Garner: "It won't work, Jack. The weak banks will pull down the strong." Garner replied: "They are about all down now anyway, the weak and strong. You will have to come to a deposit guarantee eventually, Cap'n."[27]

Garner turned out to be correct. When Glass's bill was on the Senate floor on May 19, 1933, Senator Arthur Vandenberg, a Republican from Michigan, offered an amendment providing for the immediate insurance of bank deposits up to $2,500. The amendment passed by a wide margin. Glass was a realist. He knew that deposit insurance was inevitable and used it to obtain enactment of his omnibus banking reform bill. Glass wrote to the president of a Virginia bank that while "I am unalterably opposed to what is ordinarily known as government guarantee.... I have closed neither my mind nor my ears to any proposal that holds any promise of helping us." Glass later said, "It was a problem from which we could not escape," and it was better to accept insurance and implement it in "a cautious and a conservative way than to have ourselves run over in a stampede."[28]

Roosevelt still objected to the Vandenberg amendment. For this and other reasons, the president and his administration did little to move the omnibus banking reform bill, thereby leaving the job to Glass. Willis later wrote: "It was an ironical development that the Glass bill, after passing through this long series of transformations and compromises, should now in its later stages find itself unaided by the administration upon which it had counted for support."[29] But public demand for deposit insurance proved irresistible. On June 16, 1933, President Roosevelt signed into law the Glass-Steagall Act, which, among many other matters, provided for federal insurance of bank deposits for a temporary two-year period.

The effort that Glass had launched in early 1930 for omnibus banking reform legislation finally had succeeded. Glass had had to make compromises. At the very outset, he was obliged to attempt to fix defects in the existing banking systems rather than seek to create a new system. He was required to abandon or water down some of his reform proposals, such as permitting banks to underwrite and distribute state and municipal bonds. With little direct assistance from President Roosevelt, Glass demonstrated extraordinary political skills. He utilized public concern generated by the bank holiday and the Pecora hearings (both of which he had opposed) to drive his bill forward. While Glass personally opposed deposit insurance, at the end he agreed to a limited form of insurance in order to obtain approval of his omnibus bill by both houses and the president.

Roosevelt was not far off when he described the Glass-Steagall Act as "the second most important banking legislation enacted in the history of our country." FDR certainly was correct when he congratulated Glass for obtaining enactment of a law that "had more lives than a cat."[30]

Subsequent Views of the Glass-Steagall Act

The ink was barely dry on the Glass-Steagall Act when supporters of the New Deal began hailing the act as a *New Deal* reform. In 1933, J. George Frederick termed the Glass-Steagall Act "the last of the 'New Deal' measures" enacted during the First Hundred Days of the Roosevelt Administration. In 1934, Roger W. Babson stated that although bankers did not believe that Roosevelt was in earnest when he spoke about "the money changers in the temple," the Glass-Steagall Act made them "realize it now." President Roosevelt himself, despite his adamant opposition to deposit insurance and his lukewarm support for the bill as a whole, later claimed credit for the legislation.[31]

Glass also lived to see many *anti–New Dealers* praise the separation provisions he had crafted. In 1934, James P. Warburg, an investment banker who first supported the New Deal but later broke with it, wrote: "The Glass-Steagall Bill ... contains much that is good. It provided at last the much-needed separation of the investment business from the commercial banking business."

In 1940, Samuel Pettingill, a former Democratic congressman, warned that the New Deal was moving the nation toward National Socialism and Marxism, but that there were a few positive developments, including "the divorcement of commercial and investment banking."

Perhaps the most interesting case was that of John T. Flynn. In 1933, Flynn, then a muckraking columnist for the liberal *New Republic* magazine, identified the "two good features" of the Glass-Steagall Act: "the divorcement of affiliates of banks within a year and the attempt to compel private bankers to separate their commercial-banking and investment-banking business." Flynn went on to become a vociferous anti–New Dealer and a rabid Roosevelt-hater. However, in his 1955 book, *The Decline of the American Republic,* Flynn still excoriated bank security affiliates and implicitly endorsed Glass-Steagall's separation provisions.[32]

On the other hand, during Glass's lifetime, there were those who criticized the separation provisions. In 1938, Professor George W. Edwards, chairman of the Department of Economics at New York's City College, stated that "public interest would have been better served had Congress decided to supervise rather than divorce the capital market from the commercial banking system." Edwards went on to predict that Congress would have "the inevitable task of retracing its course in the years which are yet to come."[33] Edwards's prediction came true in 1999 when Congress repealed the separation provisions.

7

GLASS'S HOSTILITY TO
THE NEW DEAL

Democrats never agree on anything, that's why they're Democrats.
If they agreed with one another, they would be Republicans.

—Will Rogers

Glass and Franklin Roosevelt knew one another from their government service during the Wilson Administration. Although Glass
was wary of FDR's unorthodox economic views, he campaigned for
his election as president in 1932. Glass's suspicions were borne out
by early New Deal laws, and he became the leading anti-New Deal
Democrat in the Senate. Glass opposed Roosevelt's unsuccessful
attempt to pack the Supreme Court and his successful bid for a third
presidential term.

Events Preceding the 1932 Presidential Campaign

Both Glass and Franklin Roosevelt had been supporters of the
Wilson Administration—Glass as a congressman, Wilson's Secretary of the Treasury, and senator; Roosevelt as Wilson's Undersecre-
tary of the Navy. Glass and Roosevelt knew one another personally.
Roosevelt was the Democrats' vice presidential candidate in 1920. In
1923, he was stricken with polio and, beginning in 1924, sought recovery in Warm Springs, Georgia. He became friendly with Georgia

12. Glass Speaks in Favor of Al Smith During the 1928 Campaign. Copyright 1928. Permission from the *Richmond Times-Dispatch*.

Democrats and other southern politicians. Some southerners saw Roosevelt as the ideal Democratic candidate for the presidency in 1928 because they wanted to block the nomination of New York governor Alfred E. Smith. They also believed that Democrats did not have much of a chance of taking the White House and Roosevelt was a respectable sacrificial lamb. Frank Freidel wrote: "Among those spreading this kind of speculative talk [about nominating Roosevelt] in 1926 was the conservative Virginian, Senator Carter Glass."[1] Roosevelt did not seek the nomination, which went to Smith, who ran against the Republican nominee, Herbert Hoover, former Secretary of Commerce in the Harding and Coolidge Administrations.

Smith faced an uphill battle because of the prosperity enjoyed by much of the nation. Moreover, Smith's connection to the New York City political machine, Tammany Hall, his support for the repeal of prohibition, and, above all, his Catholic religion made him anathema to many southern Democrats. Glass, ever the loyal Democrat, vigorously supported Smith's candidacy. Glass once remarked, "The Democratic party, at its worst, is better than the Republican party at its best."[2] Glass opposed attacks on Smith because of his Catholic religion, stressing that, "Thomas Jefferson, the founder of the Democratic Party, considered the greatest Virginian that ever breathed, was the founder of religious freedom."[3] Glass delivered a national radio address supporting Smith's candidacy. Smith went on to suffer a huge defeat, including losing Virginia and other southern states that previously had voted Democratic.

In 1928 Glass, a conservative, had been willing to back Roosevelt, a liberal, for the Democratic presidential nomination because it seemed unlikely that any Democrat could win, and Roosevelt would be a respectable loser. In contrast, as the 1932 presidential election approached, Glass believed that the deepening depression meant that the Democrats were very likely to win the White House. Glass felt that the nation needed a leader who had conservative principles and who would not seek to address the Depression with paternalistic

13. Glass Mourns Loss of the Democrats' 1932 Sound Currency Plank. Copyright 1936. Washington *Evening Star*. Used with permission.

remedies. He feared that Roosevelt, then governor of New York, did not possess these qualities. Therefore, Glass opposed Roosevelt's nomination and instead supported Newton D. Baker, who had been Secretary of War in the Wilson Administration. After the Democrats nominated Roosevelt, Glass campaigned on Roosevelt's behalf, including delivering a nationwide radio address. As discussed in Chapter 5, many observers regarded it as the best speech of the entire campaign, and Roosevelt was profuse in his thanks to Glass.

Roosevelt made a number of economically conservative statements during the campaign, but they failed to quell Glass's suspicions. After Roosevelt's overwhelming election, Glass became even more concerned. He wrote to New Hampshire Republican senator George H. Moses, who had lost his seat in the landslide: "The Democratic victory last Tuesday was too great for comfort. I am afraid it portends much trouble for those of us at Washington who want to see sane things done and insane things prevented. You may solace yourself with the reflection that you will be free from responsibility in a period of almost insuperable difficulties." Glass wrote another correspondent: "The victory Tuesday was almost too overwhelming to be safe. I hope Roosevelt will have the good sense to select a strong cabinet; otherwise he is lost."[4]

In fact, when Roosevelt began assembling his cabinet, he offered the position of Secretary of the Treasury to Glass. Glass declined the offer, partly for health reasons involving both himself and his wife, partly because he was reluctant to leave the Senate, but also because he was not satisfied with FDR's positions on monetary matters. In his public statement Glass said, "The simple fact is that I prefer to remain in the Senate because nobody has shaken my conviction that I can be of more usefulness there to the country and to the incoming administration than at the Treasury."[5] Glass's suspicions were soon confirmed.

Just one month after Roosevelt's inauguration Glass wrote to Willis, now an economics professor at Columbia University:

"More and more, I am completely satisfied with having declined to go to the Treasury. I am sure I would have found it absolutely necessary to resign in a short while had I gone there."[6]

Glass and New Deal Measures

As discussed in Chapter 6, one of the new president's first acts in March 1933 was to close all of the banks in the country for four days, citing as his authority a World War I measure, the Trading-with-the-Enemy Act. President Hoover's attorney general had advised Hoover that the act had expired at the end of the war. Glass was of the same opinion and believed that even if the act was still in force, the federal government lacked the authority to close state-chartered banks that were not members of the Federal Reserve System. However, Glass kept his reservations to himself. Next, Glass and Roosevelt had differences over the Emergency Banking Act and the Glass-Steagall Act. These differences were relatively minor and did not represent a major split on policy. So again, Glass did not go public with his criticisms of the president's policies.

14. Glass Can't Distinguish the United States and Soviet Russia. Copyright 1933. Washington *Evening Star*. Used with permission.

However, when the Roosevelt Administration turned to monetary policy, Glass publicly parted ways with the president. Glass regarded the convertibility of United States currency into gold as "the very root and definition of all business activity and confidence."[7] In direct opposition to Glass's beliefs, the Roosevelt Administration took a number of steps during its First Hundred Days designed to leave the gold standard in order to encourage inflation as an antidote to the Depression. When Roosevelt declared the bank holiday in early March 1933, he also imposed a temporary moratorium on gold payments by banks and the Treasury Department. When the bank holiday ended, the president continued the gold embargo indefinitely. In April, Senator Elmer Thomas of Oklahoma offered an amendment to the administration's Agricultural Adjustment bill that authorized the president to pursue inflationary measures including the monetization of silver, devaluation, and the issuance of greenbacks. In addition, the amendment directed the Secretary of the Treasury to encourage the Federal Reserve System to purchase more government securities on the open market. President Roosevelt endorsed the Thomas amendment.

While Glass had held his tongue over the bank holiday, the temporary moratorium on gold payments, and its indefinite continuation, he could not contain himself when Roosevelt supported the Thomas amendment. Glass delivered a major address on the Senate floor in which he argued that devaluation of the dollar not only would ruin the nation's credit and discourage investment, but that reducing the gold content of U.S. currency would "mean dishonor" and would be "immoral." Glass also alleged that any legislation requiring the Federal Reserve System to purchase government securities would convert the Fed from an independent body "into a mere agency of the Treasury Department, to be dominated by the Secretary of the Treasury."[8]

Glass's speech on April 27, 1933, his first public disagreement with the Roosevelt Administration, was hailed by much of the press.

However, Glass failed to prevent congressional enactment of the Thomas amendment. Indeed, the Roosevelt Administration went on to sponsor a resolution that voided clauses in *all* existing and future contracts, public and private, that required payment in gold. Glass objected to the resolution, claiming that it was both immoral and unconstitutional. However, the resolution was passed by Congress and signed into law by Roosevelt.

Glass's dispute with the Roosevelt Administration over monetary policy was just the first of his many public clashes with New Deal policies. Glass opposed both of the major recovery laws that were enacted during the First Hundred Days of the New Deal, the Agricultural Adjustment Act and the National Industrial Recovery Act because they were directly at odds with Glass's lifelong opposition to an activist federal government. The Agricultural Adjustment Act was designed to restore farmers' purchasing power to parity with the period 1909–1914, which had been very good years for farmers. The legislation sought to accomplish this by providing subsidies to farmers in exchange for their voluntarily decreasing production. Glass criticized the bill, stating, "There is no human being who has ever been created by God upon whom I would confer the authority and the power that this bill undertakes to confer upon the Secretary of Agriculture."[9] Congress went on to approve the bill, with Glass being one of only four Democratic senators to vote against approval.

The major break between Glass and the Roosevelt Administration occurred as a result of the administration's introduction of the National Industrial Recovery Act. The act was designed to promote national economic stability and increase profits by requiring businesses to organize on an industry basis with oversight by the National Recovery Administration under Codes of Fair Competition. Codes were required to specify maximum hours and minimum wages and to give workers the right to organize unions and to engage in collective bargaining. Cooperation under the act was exempted from prosecution under the existing antitrust laws.

15. Glass as a Possible Candidate for the Republican Presidential Nomination. 1935. Used with permission from the *Richmond Times-Dispatch*.

Glass wrote to Congressman James M. Beck: "The so-called 'Recovery Act' is not only unconstitutional, but it has been administered with a degree of brutality that has created a reign of terror and put industry, and even individual business, in involuntary servitude."[10] When he voted against the act, Glass termed it "Arbitrary, senseless, and brutal." After the NIRA was enacted, Glass congratulated newspaper columnist Walter Lippmann on his criticism of the act, "I shall always be glad of having voted against the wretched law.... I am glad, as I am sure you will ever be, that you have the courage to pungently describe the utterly dangerous effort of the federal government at Washington to transplant Hitlerism to every corner of this nation."[11]

Glass then literally put his money where his mouth was by refusing to have the newspapers that he owned affiliate with the NRA (although they did voluntarily adhere to the requirements set forth in the publishers' code). Glass wrote to Hugh Johnson, the head of the NRA (whose symbol was a blue eagle), "I just want to tell you, General, that your blue buzzard will not fly from the mastheads of my two newspapers."[12]

In addition to his disputes with the Roosevelt Administration over monetary policy and his opposition to the Agricultural Adjustment Act and the National Recovery Act, Glass opposed most other New Deal reform measures since they greatly increased the federal government's authority. In 1937, he wrote to a correspondent, "I regard the [Social Security] act literally as a Frankenstein." In 1938, he wrote to a Virginia constituent, "The whole W.P.A. [Works Progress Administration] is a frightfully expensive fraud upon the tax-payers of the country." In 1939, Glass wrote to a correspondent, "I think the National Labor Relations Act the worst law ever put on the federal statute book, and would gladly vote for its repeal or its modification in any respect."[13]

Glass's private comments regarding the New Deal were even more vitriolic. Over the years, he wrote personal letters that stated:

"It looks to me as if Hoover carried the country to the edge of the precipice and this administration is shoving it over as fast as it can. I predict the righteous failure of every damned project that these arbitrary little bureaucrats are vainly endeavoring to put into effect"; the New Deal is a series of "insane experiments"; "the policies pursued are not only futile but extremely dangerous"; "the federal government [is] protruding its nose into all kinds of business"; "it seems perfectly futile to advocate in Washington anything of a sane nature"; "mad schemes ... are constantly being projected here"; the Roosevelt Administration "seems to be utterly ignorant of the consequences of the things it advocates"; "nearly all sane persons participate in your dismay at the wasteful expenditures of this administration; but there seems to be no possible way of preventing national bankruptcy"; and "The Administration at Washington entertains an inveterate hatred of business men generally."[14]

Glass was equally hard on Democrats and Congress for going along with New Deal measures. In 1935, he wrote to a correspondent, "the pity is that the Democrats have deserted the Democratic party principles." In 1936, he wrote to Senator Millard E. Tydings about "a Congress that supinely delegated all of its constitutional authority to the President." In 1937, he wrote to another correspondent, "As matters are now, Congress is practically a rubber stamp for the Executive, and under the proposed reorganization scheme the President would have no use even for a rubber stamp; he could do his own rubber stamping."[15]

On the other hand, there were a few instances where Glass did back New Deal measures. A notable example was the creation of the Tennessee Valley Authority in 1933. The federal government had spent huge sums in developing plants in Alabama to produce nitrate, which was vital in wartime. Glass felt that these expenditures, plus the provision of cheap electricity and fertilizer to Americans living in the Tennessee Valley, more than justified continued government control. As might be expected, Glass also supported New Deal measures

16. Glass and President Roosevelt Shaking Hands. First appeared in *Carter Glass: Unreconstructed Rebel*, James E. Palmer, Jr., 1938.

aimed at cutting government spending.

More generally, Glass wrote of the "miserable New Deal" and the "abominable New Deal," and stated, "The New Deal, taken in all, is not only a mistake; it is a disgrace to the nation." In a press interview, Glass declared, "I've no objection to recognizing [Communist] Russia. We've so far beyond Russia that I am amused that Russia is willing to recognize us."[16] Glass was even mentioned as a possible Republican presidential candidate in 1936.

Court Packing

In 1936, Roosevelt was elected to a second term in a landslide election against the Republican governor of Kansas, Alfred M. Landon. Roosevelt received 60.4 percent of the popular vote and carried all but two states, Maine and Vermont. Democratic congressional candidates rode FDR's coattails. The Democrats gained six Senate seats for a record total of seventy-six Democratic senators. Democrats also gained twelve seats in the House of Representatives for a record high of 331 Democrats to 117 Republicans.[17] Conservative prospects looked bleak.

Roosevelt then committed a colossal political blunder that re-energized Republicans and conservative Democrats. Beginning in 1935, the Supreme Court struck down a series of New Deal laws, including the National Industrial Recovery Act, the Agricultural Adjustment Act, and the Guffey Coal Act, as well as a New York State minimum wage law. Roosevelt was outraged that core reform measures, overwhelmingly supported by the public and members of Congress, were being invalidated by "nine old men." He first considered seeking an amendment to the Constitution that would limit the court's jurisdiction but concluded that the necessary ratification by three-fourths of the states would take too long. FDR decided to seek legislation that would enlarge the court by providing that the president could appoint an additional justice when a sitting justice with ten or more years of service did not retire within six months following his seventieth birthday. FDR's "court-packing" plan produced an outpouring of opposition, not only from Republicans and conservative Democrats but also from many liberals.

Not surprisingly, Glass told a reporter, "Of course I shall oppose it [the plan]. I shall oppose it with all the strength which remains to me, but I don't imagine for a minute that it'll do any good. Why, if the President asked Congress to commit suicide tomorrow they'd do it." He wrote to fellow Virginia Senator Harry Byrd that Roosevelt's court-packing plan was "vindictiveness run mad."[18]

Glass spent twenty days preparing a speech criticizing the plan. Against his doctor's orders, he got up from his sickbed to deliver it as an hour-long radio address. Glass opened: "I am speaking tonight from the depths of a soul filled with bitterness against a proposition which appears to me utterly destitute of moral sensibility and without parallel since the foundation of the Republic." He ended by quoting from Rudyard Kipling:

> He shall break his judges if they cross his word;
> He shall rule above the law, calling on the Lord.
> Strangers of his counsel, hirelings of his pay,
> These shall deal out justice; sell—deny—delay.
> We shall take our station, dirt beneath his feet,
> While his hired captains jeer us in the street.[19]

Numerous Democrats, both liberals and conservatives, criticized Roosevelt's court-packing plan. Glass was front and center. George Wolfskill and John Hudson have written:

> As the drama unfolded, no one could touch Carter Glass for verbal artistry.... The court plan, he snarled, was 'frightful,' 'shocking,' 'brutal,' 'infamous,' 'outrageous;' it was 'sheer poppycock,' 'constitutional immorality,' and those who proposed it and supported it were 'political janizaries,' 'executive puppets,' 'amateur experimenters,' 'visionary incendiaries,' 'judicial sycophants,' 'judicial wet nurses.' Glass swore he would never vote to allow Roosevelt to crowd the Court with 'a lot of judicial marionettes to speak the ventriloquisms of the White House.' It was estimated that more than 700,000 copies of one of his radio speeches delivered early in the debate were circulated by opponents of the plan.[20]

While Glass's words were memorable, the key to the death of Roosevelt's court-packing plan was the number of liberals who opposed the president. The Senate Judiciary Committee voted against the plan and it died—the worst domestic defeat ever suffered by Roosevelt and the New Deal.

Roosevelt's Third Term

In 1940, Roosevelt sought the Democratic nomination for an unprecedented third presidential term. Glass was opposed to Roosevelt's attempt because of the battle over court-packing, Roosevelt's effort to purge conservative Democrats in the 1938 elections, and the president's fight over patronage with the Virginia Democratic political regime.[21] Glass backed the nomination of James Farley, Roosevelt's Postmaster General and chairman of the Democratic National Committee, who had managed Roosevelt's extremely successful campaign for a second term in 1936. Before leaving for the Democratic convention in Chicago, Farley called Glass to see if he would nominate him as planned. Glass replied, "It's a fight, ain't it, try to keep me away" and "Nothing can stop me, and I mean nothing."[22]

Glass placed Farley's name in nomination at the convention, taking a pointed slap at Roosevelt by declaring that Farley was "a man who believes in the unwritten law of the Democratic Party, as advocated ever since before the days of Thomas Jefferson, who less than three years before his death appealed to the party which he established never to nominate a man to the third term for the presidency."[23] Roosevelt was easily nominated on the first ballot with 946½ votes. Farley came in a distant second with 72½ votes. Glass then announced his intention to vote for Roosevelt in the general election. However, as in 1936, Glass did not play an active role in Roosevelt's campaign.

Glass's Personal Relationship with Roosevelt

While Glass opposed the vast majority of New Deal measures, FDR's attempt to pack the Supreme Court, and his nomination for a third term, he and the president maintained a decent working relationship. In fact, at the conclusion of his first open assault on New Deal policies, his Senate speech criticizing the administration's inflationary program, Glass stated, "It is painful to disagree with the occupant of the White House, whom I love and respect, and who has exhibited unparalleled courage in trying to bring the Government within its budgetary requirements."[24]

In both 1934 and 1935, Glass addressed Virginia's Young Democrats, praising Roosevelt's good intentions and emphasizing his friendship with the president, despite the fact that he was critical of the New Deal. Glass refused to join efforts to block Roosevelt's re-nomination in 1936 and quietly supported his re-election against the Republican challenger, Kansas governor Alfred M. Landon. On July 4, 1936, Glass introduced the president at his talk at Monticello, Virginia, Thomas Jefferson's home. Glass's remarks were largely devoted to Jefferson, but he went out of his way to praise FDR's "incomparable courage and patience in dealing with public problems" and noted that Roosevelt "professes the humanitarianism and the love of the plain people which Thomas Jefferson manifested throughout his life." Shortly thereafter, Glass tersely explained his support for FDR's re-election over Landon: "Roosevelt is a first-rate New Dealer and Landon is a third-rate New Dealer."[25]

Roosevelt reciprocated in the way he treated Glass. On April 14, 1934, Glass entered the president's office. FDR greeted him warmly, coining the phrase that was to become Glass's hallmark, "Hello, you unreconstructed old rebel." In August 1935, the president invited Glass to the White House. There, he expressed his hope that Glass would be "unanimously renominated and unanimously re-elected to the Senate," and predicted that Glass's opponent would "get about ninety votes."[26]

Various explanations have been offered as to why Glass and Roosevelt were careful not to criticize each other publicly. One of Glass's biographers, James Palmer, maintained that they respected one another's honesty, "The two men understood each other from the start. Each knew that the other was diametrically opposed to him in political philosophy but that he was honest in his convictions." Another writer, James Patterson, believed that the two men simply liked one another, "Glass, in spite of his opposition to many New Deal policies, maintained a grudging personal affection for his charming Chief Executive, a feeling which Roosevelt generally reciprocated." Senator Kenneth McKellar of Tennessee offered a similar explanation, "I do not suppose any Democratic Senator has ever differed more with the President ... than has Carter Glass.... Yet [when] he is called in, the President calls him Carter and it is a delight to hear them talk to each other. They are both fine at repartee, and the utmost good humor has always prevailed when I have seen them together."[27]

It does appear that, in the early years of Roosevelt's presidency, the two men genuinely liked one another. This is evidenced by an exchange of letters in which they joked about their differences over the gold embargo. In December 1933, Glass underwent major dental work that required the use of gold. The president wrote Glass: "I have been meaning for weeks to write you to tell you how sorry I am you had so much trouble with the teeth, and to assure you that the Attorney General will overlook the gold hoarding of which Cary Grayson [Glass's physician] says you undoubtedly have been guilty." Glass replied with equal good humor, "My dentist experienced no little difficulty in getting a sufficient amount to make the required plates; but it is hoped that before long this deficiency will also be cured." In 1934, Roosevelt and Glass were traveling together in Virginia and the president remarked, "Carter, for once I have you going along with me." Glass replied, "Yes, Franklin, for once you are going in the right direction." They were heading south. In late 1935, Glass wrote to a correspondent that, despite their political differences, President Roosevelt and he had "been personal friends for twenty-five years and are still personal friends."[28]

Whether or not the two men respected each other's honesty or genuinely liked one another, the key to their public behavior was that both were excellent politicians. It was simply smart politics not to get into a public brawl with another popular elected official, particularly one who was likely to keep getting re-elected. Roosevelt was extremely popular in Virginia. In 1935, the *New York Times* quoted one resident as stating that in the upcoming 1936 presidential election, "Roosevelt couldn't possibly lose Virginia. Every section of the State has been so well watered with Federal benefits and Federal money that potential votes lie out there in bunches."

It would have been foolhardy for Glass to criticize a president publicly who was so popular in Glass's home state. Equally, the Virginia constitution, which severely limited voting by black citizens and poorer white citizens, and the powerful state Democratic machine virtually guaranteed Glass his seat in the Senate. After Glass's appointment to the Senate in 1919, "he was elected like clockwork with the backing of the Virginia Democratic organization and his own sizable patronage following. Glass ... never made a real campaign for office and has usually been re-elected without opposition."[29] It would have made no sense for Roosevelt to attack publicly a senator who had a lock on his seat. The two men knew that they had better try to live together, and they did.

Developments in the late 1930s—including the court-packing episode, Roosevelt's attempt to purge conservative Democratic senators, and his campaign for a third term—led to a far more difficult relationship between the two men. Still, for the most part, Glass did not go public with his increasing dislike of the president. In November 1938, Glass wrote to Rixey Smith, who was writing a biography of Glass, "I desire again to caution you to let nothing of a personal nature go in the book that would betoken my intense hostility to

Mr. Roosevelt. My animosity is very bitter and very real. But I do not think it should appear in a biography." This attitude was in keeping with Glass's view that, as a loyal Democrat, he should do nothing that would result in "furnishing the Republicans with a campaign document beyond any comfort that may be derived from my public condemnation of the fool things done by this administration."[30] While Glass opposed the vast majority of New Deal measures since they expanded federal authority, he always voted for Democrats. In October 1936, he wrote to a correspondent, "you may be sure that I intend to vote the Democratic ticket at the ensuing Presidential election. This I have always done and trust I always will do. I believe strictly in party regularity and in fighting our battles within the party lines."[31]

In the late 1930s, Glass and Roosevelt were brought closer together by the darkening scene overseas. Early on, Glass had called for efforts to check Nazi Germany. He supported repeal of the arms embargo, the peacetime draft, and lend-lease. He was publicly far more hawkish than the Roosevelt Administration and wrote, "I favor selling to England, France and Poland all the munitions or anything else they may be able to buy from us;" "I would like to see England and France shoot Hitler off the map"; "we ... cannot but soon prepare this country to meet the aggressions of the mad-man in Europe"; and "I'm in favor of doing anything that would beat hell out of Hitler."[32] Roosevelt reciprocated, telling Glass, "Well, it took a war to get us together again. I hope it will take an earthquake to separate us."

Despite their past differences, FDR supported Glass's appointment in 1941 to the Senate Foreign Relations Committee, where Glass helped obtain enactment of lend lease. Whereas in the past the president had angered Glass by appointing Virginians as federal judges without conferring with the senator, Roosevelt now invited Glass to meet with him to discuss judicial appointments.[33]

Glass and Roosevelt's political rapprochement was reflected in their personal correspondence. In early 1941, the president informed Glass that the Rumanian press had identified each of them as a

"Jewish Freemason." Glass replied to FDR that this gave him great pleasure, and also that he was taking "a secret satisfaction in the apparent fact that I have gotten ahead of you for once in a fairly long lifetime, having recently been given a formal citation by a national organization of Jews and Gentiles for my outstanding religious tolerance."[34]

Glass was elected to a fourth full senatorial term in 1940, but old age and illness caused him to be largely absent from the Senate. Roosevelt's press secretary was overjoyed when in late 1944 Glass told him that he was going to vote for Roosevelt's election to a fourth term.[35]

8
GLASS AND THE FEDERAL SECURITIES LAWS

For bankers generally, the Securities and Exchange Commission is the *enfant terrible* of the Franklin D. Roosevelt era.

—U. V. Wilcox

In 1913, the Pujo subcommittee recommended legislation that would impose federal regulation on securities activities. Congress did not take action until the beginning of the New Deal. In 1933, it enacted legislation requiring corporate issuers of securities to provide disclosures to investors. Glass did not play any role with respect to that legislation. In 1934, Congress enacted legislation providing for regulation of securities exchanges. Glass was responsible for provisions creating a new federal agency, the Securities and Exchange Commission, to administer both the 1933 and 1934 laws.

The Pujo Subcommittee's Report and the Owen Bill

As mentioned in Chapter 3, in 1912 the House Committee on Banking and Currency was divided into two subcommittees. One subcommittee, chaired by Glass, was to draft reserve banking legislation, legislation that was enacted in 1913 as the Federal Reserve Act. The other subcommittee, chaired by committee chairman Arsène Pujo, was to investigate the alleged Money Trust. The Pujo subcommittee's report, drafted by its counsel, Samuel Untermyer, recommended that the nation's stock exchanges be required to adopt a series of specified rules. For example, the rules would require corporations whose securities were listed on the exchange to file specified disclosures with the exchange that would be open to public inspection and use. In addition, new exchange rules would require purchasers of securities listed on the exchange to post at least 20 percent of the price as their margin down payment. The Pujo subcommittee's report stated that Congress had the authority to impose these requirements as a result of its constitutional jurisdiction over interstate commerce and use of the mails. The report was accompanied by a draft bill implementing these requirements and placing regulatory authority in the Post Office Department.

Later in 1913, Senator Owen introduced legislation, drafted by Untermyer, embodying these recommendations.[1] As might be expected, Owen's bill was opposed by the New York Stock Exchange. More important, President Wilson declined to lend his support. Wilson was concerned over economic conditions and did not want to erode business confidence. Wilson made it clear that he would only support measures that had been part of the Democrats' 1912 platform, and securities reform had not been part of that platform.[2] While federal securities legislation was not enacted in the early twentieth century, a number of states did enact "blue sky" laws regulating securities activities in those states.

Alternative Approaches to Securities Regulation—Merit Requirements Versus Disclosure

Public interest in securities reform was put on hold during the First World War. After the war, in the final years of the Wilson Administration, there were two different types of legislative proposals for federal government regulation of corporate securities public offerings.

On January 30, 1919, Congressman John Marvin Jones, a Texas

Democrat, introduced a bill that would have required prospective corporate issuers of securities to file offering plans with the Federal Trade Commission. The bill followed the pattern of "merit regulation" used in many states. It gave the FTC the power to permit the sale of securities only if it found that the sale would be "fairly and honestly conducted both to the corporation and the public." That same day, Congressman Thomas Taylor, a Democrat from Colorado, introduced a bill requiring issuers of securities to file specified information with the Secretary of the Treasury. The Taylor bill was a disclosure measure rather than a merit regulation bill.[3] As discussed in Chapter 4, Glass, then Secretary of the Treasury, ordered the preparation of the Taylor bill as part of his battle with New York securities firms that were trying to persuade investors to sell U.S. government Bonds and invest the proceeds in new issues of corporate securities they were underwriting.[4] Thus Glass was responsible for the first securities disclosure bill introduced in Congress.

Neither the Jones bill nor the Taylor bill moved through Congress. The Wilson Administration and its allies in Congress were preoccupied with the Treaty of Versailles. Domestic reform no longer was a priority.

The Coming of the New Deal

During the bull market of the 1920s and the Harding, Coolidge, and Hoover Administrations, there was little interest in subjecting securities activities to any type of federal regulation. The 1929 stock market crash, the onset of the Great Depression, and the 1932 Pecora hearings' revelations of stock market abuses revived interest in this area.

The Democrats' 1932 platform called for legislation involving both securities disclosure and stock exchange regulation. The platform proposed "requiring to be filed with the government and carried in advertisements of all offerings of foreign and domestic stocks and bonds true information as to bonuses, commissions, principal invested, and the interest of the sellers," as well as "Regulation to the full extent of federal power, of ... Exchanges in securities and commodities."[5]

The Democrats' presidential candidate, Franklin Delano Roosevelt, was personally committed to securities reform. He often spoke about a small New York village where allegedly 110 out of 125 families were badly hurt by the 1929 stock market crash, and Roosevelt placed responsibility on investment bankers and the New York Stock Exchange. During the campaign, Roosevelt called for the enactment of legislation that would require "truth telling" in the sale of securities in order "to prevent the issue of manufactured and unnecessary securities of all kinds that are brought out merely for the purpose of enriching those who handle their sale to the public," and declared that "with respect to legitimate securities the sellers shall tell the uses to which the money is to be put." Roosevelt also called for "the use of Federal authority in the regulation of ... exchanges."[6]

However, FDR did not provide details, for example, whether securities legislation should include merit standards or follow a purely disclosure approach, and whether exchange legislation should provide solely for governmental regulation or for a combination of government regulation and self-regulation by the exchanges. Nor did Roosevelt specify which agency of the federal government—the Post Office Department, the Treasury Department, the Federal Trade Commission, or another agency—should administer the securities and stock exchange programs.

The Securities Act of 1933

After the 1932 election, President-elect Roosevelt and his advisers considered a number of approaches. First, Roosevelt's aide, Raymond Moley, asked Samuel Untermyer, who had been counsel to the Pujo subcommittee twenty years before, to draft legislation dealing with *both* securities disclosure and exchange regulation. Moley believed that Untermyer "beyond dispute, had more knowledge and more constructive ideas about [securities] reform than anyone else." However, the bill that Untermyer prepared had a fatal defect. As Moley wrote, "This bill would have placed the regulatory machinery in the Post Office Department, an obvious attempt to guarantee the measure's constitutionality. I had told Untermyer—and Roosevelt agreed—that it would be unwise to burden what was essentially a service organization with such a complex system of regulation.... Untermyer, however, did not agree."[7]

Second, unknown to Moley, the president asked Attorney General Cummings and Commerce Secretary Roper to prepare securities legislation. They contacted Huston Thompson, a former chairman of the Federal Trade Commission, an existing large federal agency, to draft a bill. The Thompson bill dealt only with the sale of securities, did not address regulation of the exchanges, and lodged regulatory jurisdiction in the Federal Trade Commission. Although the Thompson bill, like the original Taylor bill ordered by Glass in 1919, generally was a disclosure law, it had elements of merit regulation. Specifically, the Thompson bill gave the FTC the power to revoke the registration of any security if it appeared that the issuer is in "unsound condition or insolvent ... [or] when the enterprise or business of the issuer ... is not based upon sound principles, and ... the revocation is in the interest of the public welfare."[8] The Thompson bill was sharply criticized both by the business, banking, and legal communities and by *supporters* of the New Deal, such as the *New Republic*, who called it "loosely drawn and entirely inadequate."[9]

While Roosevelt initially wanted legislation that would cover *both* new securities offerings and exchange regulation, it became obvious that Untermyer and Thompson could not work together in developing such broad legislation. This meant that, in its early days, the administration was only able to develop a measure that dealt with the regulation of new securities offerings. Moley turned to Felix Frankfurter, a professor at Harvard Law School and an unofficial adviser to President Roosevelt. Frankfurter assembled a group of draftsmen including James M. Landis, another Harvard Law professor, Benjamin V. Cohen, a New York corporate lawyer, and Thomas G. Corcoran, a lawyer at the Reconstruction Finance Corporation. They drafted legislation requiring issuers of securities to file detailed registration statements with the Federal Trade Commission. It specified that investors be provided with prospectuses setting forth key information. The Landis-Cohen bill was a classic disclosure statute, along the lines of the Taylor bill that Glass had prepared in 1919 when he was Secretary of the Treasury.

A revised version of the Thompson bill was passed by the Senate, and the Landis-Cohen bill was passed by the House of Representatives. A Senate-House conference committee met to work out the final bill, which was largely based on the Landis-Cohen measure, and the final bill was passed by both houses. On May 27, 1933, President Roosevelt signed into law the first of the federal securities laws, the Securities Act of 1933.

While the Roosevelt Administration had to overcome Wall Street objections and utilize *three* separate drafting groups, Congressional passage of the Securities Act was relatively easy. This was largely because the act was taken up by Congress during the administration's First Hundred Days, when sixteen major New Deal statutes (including the Glass-Steagall Act) were enacted with great haste in the midst of the economic emergency, with little time for scrutiny by members of Congress or lobbying by interest groups. Cohen joked with Landis that Sam Rayburn, chairman of the House Interstate Commerce Committee, had said that he "did not know whether the bill passed so readily because it was so damned good or so damned incomprehensible."[10]

Although Glass had had the first federal securities disclosure bill prepared when he was Secretary of the Treasury in 1919, he did not play any role in connection with the Securities Act of 1933. In early 1933, Glass was totally preoccupied with major banking legislation, the Glass-Steagall Act, which Roosevelt signed into law in June 1933. Glass's intense focus on banking matters and complete disinterest in securities disclosure measures was underscored by his behavior as a member of the conference committee on the securities disclosure bills. Glass "unexpectedly burst into a tirade after scanning the bill, because he erroneously assumed the securities bill conflicted with his proposed Banking Act. Only after being reassured by Landis and Cohen that the House bill systematically excluded from its operations all securities issued by state or nationally chartered banks was the Virginian mollified." Once Glass learned that the securities bill would not impact his banking bill, Glass immediately left the scene: "Hastily thumbing the bill for any further reference to banks, he growled an additional warning, then departed from the Conference Committee, never to return."[11]

The Securities Exchange Act of 1934

The Roosevelt Administration next turned to the second area of securities regulation that was called for in the Democrats' 1932 platform and that FDR had advocated during the campaign—regulation of the nation's stock exchanges. Obtaining the enactment of legislation in this area was likely to be far more difficult than had been the case with the 1933 legislation regarding public offerings of securities. The emergency climate of the Roosevelt Administration's First Hundred Days was over. Members of Congress were reasserting themselves. The New York Stock Exchange possessed great financial and political power and could be expected to oppose any legislation that threatened to diminish its authority and prestige.

In classic New Deal fashion, the Roosevelt Administration began by developing two very different types of legislative proposals—one based on continued self-regulation by the exchanges with minimal oversight by the federal government, and the other providing for direct government regulation of exchange practices in key areas.

First, Roosevelt asked Secretary of Commerce Roper to head a committee to develop recommendations for a stock exchange bill. Roper turned the project over to Assistant Commerce Secretary John Dickinson. Before the committee issued its report, one member, Henry Richardson, circulated his draft legislation. It provided for the creation of a new federal agency, the Stock Exchange Commission, appointed by the president. Two of the agency's seven members would be members of exchanges. This was in keeping with the exchanges' belief that regulation should not be placed in the hands of reformers, but rather with experts on exchange practices, including exchange members themselves. Roper's report stressed that "Self-regulation should be emphasized ... and the governing boards of the exchange should, in the first instance, formulate ... fair rules, subject to the veto of the Federal Regulatory Authority." The report was so committed to self-regulation by the exchanges that it enumerated powers that the new federal agency, the Stock Exchange Commission, could *not* exercise, including licensing individual brokers; regulating non-exchange ("over-the-counter") markets; limiting margin loans; and curbing short sales.[12] Subsequently, a number of other parties, including the Twentieth Century Fund, an early think tank, and Senator King of Utah, proposed creation of a new securities agency.[13]

A very different approach was taken in legislation requested by James Landis, now a commissioner of the Federal Trade Commission, the agency that was administering the Securities Act of 1933. This legislation was drafted by Benjamin Cohen and two younger government lawyers, I. N. P. Stokes and Telford Taylor. The bill was far more complicated than the Dickinson bill, as evidenced by the fact that it had been rewritten *thirteen times* before Cohen put the bill into final form.[14] The bill did not call for the creation of a new federal agency that would only have the power to veto stock exchange rules; instead, it utilized the FTC, which was administering the Securities Act of 1933 and which was to have *direct* regulatory authority over the exchanges in critical areas such as price manipulation, segregation of broker and dealer functions, and the power to set margin requirements higher than those specified in the bill.

The Landis-Cohen bill was introduced in both houses of Congress. It was greeted with a firestorm of criticism. The New York Stock Exchange organized opposition from brokerage firms, regional stock exchanges, and corporations whose securities traded on exchanges. The regional stock exchanges, who were particularly effective in lobbying since they were located in cities across the country, contacted their senators and representatives. The attacks on the bill got ugly, including claims the bill's proponents were radicals or communists. Joseph P. Kennedy later wrote that the bill "was assailed as state socialism and regimentation; and, in accordance with the custom of parading imaginary horribles, it was prophesied that the securities markets of the country would dry up within a few months." Will Rogers observed that "Those old Wall Street boys are putting up an awful fight to keep the government from putting a cop on their corner."[15]

The wave of criticism drove the New Dealers back to the drawing board. President Roosevelt was personally involved in the effort to revise the bill and became its most effective advocate. The revised bill softened many provisions dealing with exchange structure and practices. The bill moved jurisdiction over investors' use of margin from the FTC to the Federal Reserve Board. This outraged Glass, who did not want the Fed involved with the stock market, including setting margin, stating, "In my opinion not one of the eight board members knows anything about it. The Federal Reserve Board was set up to respond to the requirements of credit, not to control credit."[16]

The bill still utilized the FTC, rather than a new federal agency, as the regulator of stock exchange practices. Ben Cohen wrote that the New Dealers "fought against ... [creation of a new agency] because experience had indicated that commissions in time tend to be dominated by those they regulate and ... a commission that had other tasks than stock exchange tasks and security tasks might be less the prisoner of the financial community."[17]

The revisions failed to satisfy the exchanges, who continued to vigorously oppose both the bill's substantive provisions and its designation of the FTC as the regulatory agency. Sam Rayburn, chairman of the House Interstate Commerce Committee, stated that the revised bill was being attacked by "the most vicious and persistent lobby that any of us have ever known in Washington."[18]

The complexity of the policy issues can be illustrated by briefly considering one issue: investors purchasing securities with borrowed money, commonly referred to as "buying on margin." There was a widespread belief that the use of excessive low margin buying had been a major contributor to the severity of the 1929 crash and that the key to reform was setting limits on margin purchases. For example, President Roosevelt told Secretary of the Treasury Henry Morgenthau that "Speculative trading must be very greatly curtailed, [and] that means ... a much smaller volume of trading on the ... exchanges; it means also of necessity the requirement of very large margins and sufficient flexibility in some agency of government to increase margin requirements if the minimum amount provided in the bill itself does not in practice greatly curtail speculative trading."[19] However, there was no agreement as to how any new law should address this problem. For example, should rigid percentage limits on margin be set forth in the statute itself, or left to the exchanges, or delegated to the regulatory agency, or given to the usual regulator of money and credit, the Federal Reserve Board?

Glass Steps In

As discussed in Chapter 4, when Carter Glass served as Secretary of the Treasury, he stated that the New York Stock Exchange was in need of reform, and that if the exchange did not proceed on its own, government should take action. However, in 1934 Glass, by then a senator, was focused on banking issues and the Federal Reserve System, and initially evinced little interest in legislation dealing with stock exchanges. Ironically, Glass's focus on the Fed led him to play a critical role in the development of stock exchange legislation.

The Roosevelt Administration's revised bill provided that the Federal Trade Commission was to be the regulatory authority, but that control over margin would be lodged in the Federal Reserve Board. Glass vigorously objected to the Fed having margin authority. Glass offered an amendment that would abolish the jurisdiction of both the FTC and the Fed and that would create a new three-person Securities Exchange Commission.

Glass's amendment was designed to kill *three* birds with one stone.

First, it would carry out Glass's goal of keeping the Fed away from any involvement with the stock market.

Second, Glass believed that margin limits should not be set in stone in statute and should be left to an agency, but that the FTC lacked the expertise to set margin limits as needed. A columnist in the *Washington Post* described Glass's position this way: "He proposed to put the regulatory powers in the hands of a special commission and leave it to the commission to determine from time to time what marginal [sic] requirements should be. His own view was that the Federal Trade Commission ... is singularly devoid of the practical experience and knowledge essential for competent administration of such law."[20] Senator Alben Barkley of Kentucky shared Glass's skepticism about use of the FTC—adding a securities department to the FTC would merely be "sort of a lean-to under the [Federal Trade] commission's original activities."[21]

Third, Glass's amendment providing for a new federal agency would mollify the New York Stock Exchange and others in the business community who feared excessive regulation of the exchanges by New Deal reformers at the FTC. The Senate committee, over the objections of both the Roosevelt Administration and committee chairman Fletcher, adopted Glass's amendment creating a new agency by a 10-to-8 vote.

Meanwhile, President Roosevelt and his closest allies in Congress continued to oppose creation of a new agency. In violation of Congressional tradition, Fletcher did not name senior committee members Glass and Robert Wagner to the Senate-House conference committee on the exchange legislation since both favored creation of a new agency. Nearly simultaneously, Roosevelt informed a press conference that he "personally" preferred use of the Federal Trade Commission.

Glass resigned from the Senate Banking Committee in a huff, stating that the decision not to name him to the conference committee was "a direct affront and a gratuitous indignation, and deliberately intended to be." Glass also criticized the president for breaking his alleged promise to support creation of a new agency. Senator Barkley, a close friend of Glass, offered to give up his seat on the conference committee. The Senate Majority Leader, Senator Robinson, refused to accept either resignation. Roosevelt hastily beat a retreat, telling the press that it was "not a frightfully important thing, one way or the other," which government agency was used.[22]

The reorganized conference committee adopted Glass's position that the legislation should create a new agency, changing its name from the Securities Exchange Commission to the Securities and Exchange Commission, and changing its composition from three to five members. However, the conference committee rejected Glass's goal of placing authority over margin in the SEC and instead gave margin authority to the Fed.

On June 6, 1934, President Roosevelt signed into law the Securities Exchange Act of 1934. The act created a new federal agency, the U.S. Securities and Exchange Commission, to administer the Securities Act of 1933 as well as the new 1934 act. The law placed authority over margin in the Federal Reserve Board.

The actions of many individuals and groups contributed to the terms of the final legislation, including the provisions that created the SEC. Alfred Cash Koeniger has asserted: "Virtually single-hand-edly, Glass was responsible for the creation of the Securities and Exchange Commission."[23] While this is somewhat of an exaggeration, the record demonstrates that Glass did play a critical role in the creation of the SEC.

Reflections on the Securities Exchange Act of 1934

The battle over the Securities Exchange Act was the most hard fought and bitter of any involving early New Deal measures. President Roosevelt himself observed that "a more definite and highly organized drive is being made against effective legislation [for Stock Exchange regulation] than against any similar recommendation made by me."[24]

As often is the case with major legislation, the passage of time has revealed a number of ironies.

Senator Glass proposed creation of a new government agency, the SEC, so that it, rather than the Federal Reserve Board, would have authority to establish percentage limits on margin purchases. Although the final legislation did create the SEC, the legislation placed margin authority in the Fed, just what Glass wanted to avoid.

Wall Street sought the creation of a new government agency since it feared regulation by reform-minded officials at the Federal Trade Commission. While the final legislation created a new agency, President Roosevelt went on to appoint leading FTC reform-minded officials as three of the SEC's first five commissioners.

New Dealers opposed creation of a new agency devoted solely to securities regulation since they feared that a small agency dedicated only to securities regulation could easily be dominated by Wall Street. However, this did not turn out to be the case. Justice William O. Douglas later wrote: "it seemed to me that most agencies become so closely identified with the interests they are organized to regulate, eventually they are transformed into spokesmen for the interest groups.... The SEC was not like this in the early days."[25]

New Dealers such as Roosevelt, Cohen, and Landis believed that securities regulation would be more effective if conducted by a large and well-established agency with many other responsibilities, like the Federal Trade Commission, rather than by a new specialized agency. However, experience proved otherwise. In 1938, Landis conceded that he had been wrong and stated: "By creating a new Commission... it was possible to have individuals in charge whose sole single c oncern was the problem of securities regulation. They were not thus required to dissipate their energies over a wide periphery."[26]

In 1934, creation of the SEC appeared to be a major defeat for some notable New Dealers. They had fought tooth and nail against creation of the SEC and lost. However, when the SEC turned out to be a highly well-regarded agency, New Dealers claimed it as their creation. Thus, the website of the SEC Historical Society proclaims the SEC to be "The Best New Deal Agency."[27]

Finally, Senator Glass was the leading Democratic conservative opponent of much New Deal legislation because he generally opposed an activist federal government. However, he was the person most responsible for creation of the model New Deal agency, the U.S. Securities and Exchange Commission, because he favored legislation to curb the financial sector and wanted a specialized agency to implement the program.

The Federal Reserve Building in Washington, DC, has a bas relief bust of Carter Glass, honoring him as "The Defender of the Federal Reserve System." The SEC might consider placing a similar plaque in its lobby honoring Carter Glass, "The Father of the Securities and Exchange Commission."[28]

9
GLASS AND THE BANKING ACT OF 1935

Men often oppose a thing, merely because they had no agency in planning it; or because it may have been planned by those whom they dislike.

—Alexander Hamilton

In 1934, the Roosevelt Administration drafted an omnibus banking bill. At the urging of the head of the Federal Reserve Board, Marriner S. Eccles, the bill would have strengthened the role of the board in Washington and decreased the role of the regional reserve banks. Glass, who had authored the Federal Reserve Act providing for a decentralized reserve banking system, opposed these provisions. The final legislation generally followed Eccles's proposals while retaining the system's unique federal structure.

Administration Prepares Omnibus Banking Legislation

The November 1934 Congressional elections produced a resounding vote of confidence in the Roosevelt Administration. For the first time in modern history, the president's party gained congressional seats in both houses of Congress in an off-year election. This victory gave the administration the confidence to prepare a major round of new legislative proposals.

In late 1934, immediately after the elections, the administration began developing banking legislation that was to be presented to Congress the following year. Pursuant to the president's instructions, Secretary of the Treasury Henry Morgenthau, Jr. told the Treasury's Interdepartmental Loan Committee that an administration subcommittee would be formed to develop "one ominous bill." Morgenthau asked each federal banking agency to provide its suggestions for possible inclusion. The head of one agency, Chairman Crowley of the Federal Deposit Insurance Corporation, argued that legislation involving his agency was a necessity and shouldn't be tied to other proposals that would be more difficult to enact. However, there was a general consensus among the various agency officials to develop a single banking bill. The debate between having one omnibus banking bill versus separate bills was to come up numerous times during the battle over the Banking Act of 1935.

Two of the agencies put forth suggestions for legislation that were likely to be enacted rather easily if they proceeded on their own. FDIC Chairman Crowley proposed to make FDIC insurance of bank deposits permanent, a move that would be applauded by the banking industry, which had come to support deposit insurance. Similarly, the Comptroller of the Currency, James O'Connor, wanted to extend the deadline set forth in the Glass-Steagall Act for directors of national banks either to end loans granted them by their institutions or give up their positions. This too was bound to be a popular measure with bankers. However, both officials reluctantly agreed to have their easy-to-enact provisions wrapped into an omnibus bill.

At this point, a major problem was presented by the program put forth by the new chairman (then called the governor) of the Federal Reserve Board, Marriner S. Eccles.

Marriner Eccles and His Program

Eccles came from a wealthy family in Utah. His father had created a business empire that included a large number of enterprises. Eccles expanded this empire even further, including the creation of a large banking entity, First Security Corporation. For most of his business career, Eccles had been a staunch Republican and a firm believer in *laissez faire* economics. However, the Great Depression changed his thinking completely. Eccles later wrote, "I was brought face to face with this proposition: that *the only way we could get out of the depression was through government action in placing purchasing power in the hands of people who were in need of it.*" (Emphasis in the original).[1] Eccles's ideas, which at that time were highly unorthodox for a businessman-banker and which preceded John Maynard Keynes's published works in this area, brought him to the attention of some of the early New Dealers. In February 1934, Eccles was named as a special assistant on monetary and credit issues to Secretary of the Treasury Morgenthau.

In August 1934, Morgenthau suggested to President Roosevelt that Eccles succeed Eugene Black as governor of the Federal Reserve Board. When Roosevelt interviewed him, Eccles made it clear that he would accept the nomination only if the Federal Reserve System was changed to seat power in the Federal Reserve Board in Washington, DC. Eccles believed that private banking interests had too much influence in the system through regional federal Reserve Banks, particularly the New York Reserve Bank. Eccles wanted authority centralized in the board so that it could promote economic stability through its control over monetary policy.[2]

Eccles gave the president a memorandum outlining his program. Previously, the regional reserve banks oversaw open market activities (the Fed's purchases and sales of government securities in the open market) through their *exclusive* membership on the Open Market Committee, with only loose supervision by the Federal Reserve Board. The other regional reserve banks gave great deference to one member of the Open Market Committee, the New York Federal Reserve Bank, thus giving the New York Reserve Bank the power to control the nation's money and credit. Eccles proposed granting the board exclusive control over open market activities. Eccles also wanted to give the board control over the regional Federal Reserve Banks by granting it the power to approve or disapprove the heads (then called governors) of the reserve banks who had been appointed by their own boards of directors. Eccles admitted that these measures would make the Fed more closely resemble a true central bank, while maintaining the appearance of a decentralized system, stating:

> The adoption of these suggestions would introduce certain attributes of a real central bank capable of energetic and positive action without calling for a drastic revision of the whole Federal Reserve Act. Private ownership and local autonomy are preserved but on really important questions of policy, authority and responsibility are concentrated in the Board. Thus effective control is obtained while the intense opposition and criticism that greets every central bank proposal is largely avoided.[3]

Eccles met with the President to outline his program. At the end of the meeting, FDR gave Eccles the go-ahead: "Marriner, that's quite an action program you want. It will be a knock-down and drag-out fight to get it through. But we might as well undertake it now as at any other time. It seems to be necessary."[4] A few days after the meeting, Roosevelt gave Eccles a "recess appointment" as governor of the Federal Reserve Board, meaning that he would hold the office while the Senate was on recess but would have to be confirmed by the Senate when it returned.

Eccles then presented his program to the administration's internal subcommittee that was preparing the Omnibus Banking Bill. The

Chairman of the FDIC and the Comptroller of the Currency still preferred to have separate bills limited to their respective issues, but the subcommittee continued to support introduction of a single Omnibus Banking Bill. Title I of the bill contained the FDIC provisions, Title II embodied Eccles's program for the Federal Reserve System, and Title III had the Comptroller's provisions. As Eccles stated, the administration's omnibus bill approach was based on "tying something the bankers didn't want [Title II] to something [Titles I and III] they wanted very much."[5]

Glass was unlikely to be pleased by Eccles's program since it was contrary to the thrust of the Federal Reserve Act of 1913 and its creation of a geographically *decentralized* reserve banking system. As discussed in Chapter 3, Senator Glass had played the leadership role in the development and enactment of the Federal Reserve Act, which he regarded as a nearly perfect piece of legislation. Moreover, both Eccles and Glass were extremely strong willed. Both President Roosevelt and Eccles made the situation with Glass worse. Roosevelt did not clear the appointment of Eccles as Governor of the Federal Reserve Board with Glass. Eccles did not pay a courtesy visit on Glass until two months *after* his appointment. Finally, Roosevelt and Eccles did not provide Glass with an advance copy of Eccles's proposals before the bill was introduced in Congress, as Glass believed had been promised. A clash between Eccles and Glass over the omnibus bill was inevitable.

When the administration's banking bill was introduced in Congress on February 6, 1935, the press immediately focused on Eccles's federal reserve program in Title II. Newspaper columnist Walter Lippman wrote: "The heart of the matter is the proposal to increase the powers of the Federal Reserve Board in Washington. More exactly, it is the proposal to centralize in Washington the power to expand and contract the volume of credit through the purchase and sale of government securities. This is the power to inflate and to deflate, and it is the most important power which any central banking system possesses." The headline in *Business Week* read: "'Minimum' Bank Law: Federal Reserve Board proposes to take over the [Federal Reserve] System, lock, stock, and barrel." The *Wall Street Journal* reported that, "as a whole the bill has been ingeniously drawn to set up the substance of a central bank, virtually though not technically as subdued to the will of the Administration as if the central reserve bank was legally the property of the government."[6]

The House of Representatives and the Senate took up the administration's Omnibus Banking Bill but did so in very different ways.

The Omnibus Bill in the House of Representatives

Soon after its introduction in the House, the Banking and Currency Committee, chaired by Congressman Henry Steagall of Alabama, held hearings on the bill. The hearings were stacked with favorable witnesses. Representatives of the administration, including FDIC Chairman Crowley, Comptroller of the Currency O'Connor, and Federal Reserve Board Governor Eccles, testified for a total of eighteen days, leaving only seven days for all other witnesses. The regional federal Reserve Banks, whose power would be reduced by the bill, and private New York banks, whom Eccles believed controlled the New York Reserve Bank, were not invited to testify.

Following the House hearings, Steagall introduced a revised version of the bill. The revised bill reflected Eccles's testimony by providing for even more centralization of authority in the Federal Reserve Board than the original bill. For example, open market operations were to be conducted by the Federal Reserve Board itself rather than by a committee of the board. The revised omnibus bill was reported out of the House Banking Committee and passed the House by an overwhelming vote on May 9, 1935.

The Omnibus Banking Bill in the Senate

While the omnibus banking bill had an easy time in the House, the Senate was an entirely different matter, because of Senator Glass.

When the Democrats took control of the Senate in March 1933, Glass, because of his seniority, had the choice of becoming chairman of either the Banking and Currency Committee or the Appropriations Committee. If Glass chose the Banking Committee, the chairmanship of the Appropriations Committee would go to Senator McKellar, a move the Roosevelt Administration opposed. Therefore, the Administration urged Glass to become chairman of the Appropriations Committee. Although the chairmanship of the Banking Committee had technically gone to Senator Fletcher, the Administration had promised that Glass would have actual control and would chair a subcommittee, the Subcommittee on Monetary Policy, Banking, and Deposit Insurance, which would deal with *all* banking issues.

The administration's Omnibus Banking Bill was introduced in the Senate on the same day as in the House, February 6, 1935. The bill was sent to the Committee on Banking and Currency, nominally chaired by Senator Fletcher. The administration wanted that committee itself, rather than Glass's subcommittee, to take up the bill. However, the committee voted unanimously to refer the bill to Glass's subcommittee.

Glass's strategy then relied on looming deadlines related to Titles I and III (dealing with FDIC insurance and bank loans to bank directors). If these were not enacted into law by July 1, temporary FDIC insurance of deposits would end, and many bank directors would lose their jobs because they had outstanding loans from their banks. Glass sought to delay Senate action on the bill and make Title II as controversial as possible, pressuring Congress to enact a bill limited to Titles I and III by the July 1 deadline.

Glass's first step was to announce that, while his subcommittee would hold hearings on the bill, these would not take place until the Senate first had passed a major appropriations bill then before the

Appropriations Committee. After the appropriations bill was disposed of, Glass announced that his subcommittee would next take up Eccles's nomination as governor of the Federal Reserve Board. It soon became clear that Glass intensely disliked both Eccles's program and Eccles himself. In January, Glass wrote to ex-Senator Smoot of Utah asking for information on Eccles's fitness to be governor of the board, particularly his claim to have severed all of his bank holding company connections. In February, Glass wrote to a correspondent: "The Eccles bank plan is opposed to the whole history and tradition of the Democratic Party, and it is something never attempted to be done by even a central bank of Europe." In March, he wrote in another letter: "It is a dangerous bill by a dangerous man." In April, he told H. Parker Willis, who had been his aide on both the Federal Reserve Act and the Glass-Steagall Act: "I must go on the Eccles Banking Bill and do my best to wreck it. I have some hope also of wrecking Eccles."[7]

Glass urged the members of his subcommittee to vote against confirming Eccles as governor of the Federal Reserve Board. However, the subcommittee voted 4 to 3 to confirm the appointment. The full Senate then voted to confirm, with Glass being the only senator to vote against confirmation. Recently a man with enormous potential power, Glass was becoming an increasingly isolated figure.

Having failed to defeat the provisions in the bill dealing with the Fed through delay and by blocking Eccles's confirmation, Glass was finally ready to have his subcommittee hold hearings. The hearings began on April 19, 1935, more than two months after the bill's introduction in the Senate. Whereas Congressman Steagall had stacked the House hearings with witnesses who favored Eccles's proposals, Glass loaded the Senate hearings with witnesses who were hostile to them. The first two witnesses were FDIC Chairman Crowley and Comptroller of the Currency O'Connor, who indicated that they could live with a bill that was limited to Titles I and III. The next witness was James P. Warburg of the Bank of Manhattan, who stated that Title II, dealing with the Federal Reserve System, was tantamount to the nationalization of the nation's banking system. Other bankers delivered similar testimony. Winthrop Aldrich of Chase National Bank testified that Title II "is not liberalizing the Federal Reserve System. It is making it over into an instrument of despotic authority." James H. Perkins, chairman of National City Bank testified: "Title II fundamentally changes our banking system. It places in the hands of a board the power to dictate arbitrarily the money policies of the country."[8]

A few bankers dissented from the generally hostile view of large bank witnesses. A. P. Giannini of Bank of America issued a statement directly criticizing Warburg's testimony: "However typical his attitude may be taken as that of the New York banker it by no means represents the attitude of many bankers outside New York.... Personally I would rather that this power be exercised by a public body in the public interest than by the New York banking fraternity."[9] However, as Glass intended, the vast majority of witnesses followed Warburg's lead and testified in strong opposition to the Fed centralization plan set forth in Title II of the omnibus bill.

The administration became increasingly impatient with Glass's delaying tactics and lopsided hearings. On April 28, 1935, President Roosevelt delivered a radio address on the state of the economy. FDR recited the history of the Federal Reserve System and declared, "Twenty years of experience with this System have justified the efforts made to create it, but these 20 years have shown by experience definite possibilities for improvement. Certain proposals made to amend the Federal Reserve Act deserve prompt and favorable action by the Congress. They are a minimum of wise readjustment of our Federal Reserve System in the light of past experience and present needs."[10]

The subcommittee's hearings did not end until June 3, almost four months after the bill had been introduced in Congress. Time was running out as the July 1 deadline approached. Glass hoped that first his subcommittee would report out a bill limited to Titles I and III, that then the full committee would do the same, and finally that the Senate would pass the pared-down bill by July 1.

The administration and its congressional allies fought back. They prepared a resolution extending the July 1 deadline by sixty days. Congressman Steagall introduced the resolution in the House, where it was promptly passed. The Senate then adopted the same resolution. Glass's strategy had been defeated.

Glass offered a revised bill in which Title II was totally rewritten. Helen Burns reported: "Every sentence and almost every paragraph had been changed. The... bill was greatly altered from that originally introduced and differed substantially from the legislation passed by the House of Representatives."[11] Glass's revised bill was reported out by the subcommittee and then by the full committee. It was then passed by the Senate. The House refused to go along with the Senate-passed bill. Therefore, a conference committee made up of members of the Senate and House banking committees was appointed to come up with a compromise bill. That compromise bill was passed by both houses and signed into law by President Roosevelt as the Banking Act of 1935. Just as President Wilson had done when he signed the Federal Reserve Act into law in 1913, President Roosevelt signed the Banking Act of 1935 using several pens. He then gave pens to those in the audience who had helped obtain enactment of the law. When Roosevelt gave one of the pens to Glass, someone said in a stage whisper, "He should have given him an eraser instead."[12]

The Banking Act of 1935

The final act reflected a series of compromises between Eccles's program and Glass's views.

17. President Roosevelt Signing the Banking Act of 1935 (Glass is on the far left.) Harris & Ewing, 1935. Library of Congress, Prints & Photographs Division, photograph by Harris & Ewing, [reproduction number, e.g., LC-USZ62-123456].

Composition of the Open Market Committee

Before the 1935 Act, the Open Market Committee consisted *exclusively* of representatives of the twelve Federal Reserve Banks, with *no* representation of the Federal Reserve Board. The House bill, which reflected Eccles's position, provided for an Open Market Committee consisting *exclusively* of members of the Federal Reserve Board. The Senate bill provided for an Open Market Committee consisting of all seven members of the Federal Reserve Board and five representatives of Federal Reserve Banks selected on a rotating basis. The final act adopted the Senate version. Thus, the act was a compromise between the prior situation (no Federal Reserve Board representation) and Eccles's program (exclusive board representation), but tilted toward

Eccles's position by having seven of the twelve members come from the board.

Federal Reserve Board Approval of Reserve Bank Governors

Before the 1935 Act, Governors of the regional Federal Reserve Banks were appointed by each bank's board of directors. Eccles wanted to give the Federal Reserve Board control over the regional Reserve Banks by granting it the power to approve or disapprove the banks' governors. Therefore, the administration's bill provided that governors were to be elected annually by the banks' directors, subject to approval by the Federal Reserve Board. The House bill extended the term to three years and the Senate bill to five years. The final act adopted the Senate version. Eccles won his main point, approval authority over the governors of the Federal Reserve Banks by the Federal Reserve Board, but the five-year term offered the opportunity for greater governor independence than the one-year term initially proposed by Eccles and the administration.

Composition of the Federal Reserve Board

Before the 1935 Act, the Federal Reserve Board had consisted of eight members, six appointed by the president. and two ex officio members, the Secretary of the Treasury and the Comptroller of the Currency. Eccles wanted to reduce the board to five members and eliminate the two ex officio members. The House bill left the board's composition unchanged. Glass long believed that the board's independence would be increased by deleting the Secretary of the Treasury, a political figure. Earlier, in January 1930, Glass had written to Professor Willis: "I have thought for a long time that the Secretary of the Treasury should not be a member of the Federal Reserve Board, since he has come to dominate federal reserve banking."[13] Secretary of the Treasury Morgenthau was miffed at the proposal that his position be abolished while the Comptroller of the Currency, a subordinate official in his own department, would continue. The final act deleted *both* ex officio positions and provided for a board of seven members, all appointed by the president. Here was a case where both Eccles and Glass largely got what they wanted.

Reflections on the Banking Act of 1935

Glass believed that he had been the winner in his battle with Eccles and the Roosevelt Administration over the Federal Reserve provisions in the 1935 Act. Shortly after the act was signed into law, Glass wrote to a correspondent: "We won a remarkable victory on the bank bill; and, if the President will now appoint the right sort of Board of Governors of the Federal Reserve System, the banks will get some respite from the threatenings of men of the Eccles style." In a letter to another correspondent, Glass was more pungent: "We did not leave enough of the Eccles bill with which to light a cigarette."[14] Similarly, one of Glass's biographers, Alfred Cash Koeniger, concluded that Glass's "triumph could not have been more complete."[15] On the other side, Eccles was equally convinced that he and the Roosevelt Administration were the victors.[16]

More objective writers than Glass and Eccles have concluded that the administration and Eccles were the winners. In 1935, newspaper columnist Walter Lippmann wrote: "The original bill not merely concentrated responsibility somewhere; it concentrated it in a board under the influence of the President.... the Administration strategists stood pat ... [and] let Senator Glass amend the bill.... The net result is a better bill than the original. Yet it is a bill which represents a triumph of Governor Eccles' fundamental idea." In 1974, Helen M. Burns wrote: "On the whole ... the administration was by far the greater winner." In 2003, Allan H. Meltzer wrote: "In fact, the compromise gave Eccles many of the changes he wanted. Glass lost on the shift of power to the Board, [and] the diminished powers of the regional reserve banks.... The 1935 Act permitted the Federal Reserve to become a central bank." Most recently, in 2016 Professor Conti-Brown wrote, "Eccles and FDR had created a new central banking model altogether."[17]

However, Glass's defeat was not total. While the 1935 Act cut back the authority of the regional reserve banks and enhanced the authority of the Federal Reserve Board, the Federal Reserve System (unlike European central bank schemes) still retained the unique federal structure that Glass helped create in 1913. Moreover, the act did not provide that the Open Market Committee would consist entirely of board representatives as Eccles proposed, but rather that it would have representatives of *both* the board and the regional reserve banks, reflecting the system's federal nature.

Glass's behavior during the battle over the Banking Act of 1935 left a good deal to be desired. It was standard politics for Glass to use tactics such as delay and stacked hearings to make his opposition effective. What is more troubling is that Glass appeared to be motivated as much by his own ego and his animus toward Eccles as by his beliefs about good public policy. No doubt Eccles offended Glass by not paying him an early courtesy visit and by not providing him with an advance copy of his plans. However, one senses that what really bothered Glass was that he viewed himself as the *sole* arbiter of what was good for the Federal Reserve System. Proposals regarding alterations in the system that emanated from others, even the best of proposals, were anathema to Glass. Glass had long feared Wall Street control of the nation's banking system and therefore should have shared Eccles's interest in shifting control of the Open Market Committee from the regional Federal Reserve Banks, notably the New York Federal Reserve Bank, toward the Federal Reserve Board. Yet he opposed this reform, likely because Eccles was its sponsor.

Glass's actions regarding the Banking Act of 1935 stood in sharp contrast to his behavior during the development of the Federal Reserve Act and the Glass-Steagall Act, when he was willing to accept others' ideas. Success, and possibly age, had diminished Glass's judgment. Given the Roosevelt Administration's commitment to Eccles's program and the overwhelming pro-Administration majorities in both houses, Glass would have been better-advised to work with Eccles and the administration to bring Eccles's program more to his liking, rather than seeking to prevent its enactment. The final act was not a total victory for Eccles, but the character of Glass's opposition diminished his reputation as the nation's foremost authority on banking legislation.

Glass's animus towards Eccles continued. In September 1938, he wrote a letter stating: "You are quite right in saying that the Federal Reserve Act has been flagrantly maladministered." Two months later, he wrote to another correspondent: "The Federal Reserve System is being gradually destroyed by the financial adventurer whom the President insisted upon designating as its head. Eccles has persistently sought to transform the Federal Reserve Board from a supervisory board into a Central Bank."[18]

An Odd Development

When Congress took up the Banking Act of 1935, Glass was concerned that the lack of investment capital was contributing to the continuation of the Great Depression. He therefore supported a provision that would have permitted commercial banks themselves (but not their affiliates) to underwrite (but not publicly distribute) securities, subject to a number of stringent conditions. Under Glass's proposal, a bank could underwrite an issue of corporate securities up to 10 percent of the bank's unimpaired capital and surplus. A bank could underwrite up to 20 percent of a corporate issue subject to a limit of $100,000. The total corporate underwritings of a bank at any particular time could not exceed 200 percent of the bank's unimpaired capital and surplus. Sales could not be made directly to customers of the bank or to other banks. Sales could only be made on stock exchanges and to brokers and dealers who were registered with the Securities and Exchange Commission.[19]

President Roosevelt repeatedly wrote to Glass to express his vehement personal opposition to the proposal. In July 1935, the president wrote: "You have had a long period of intimate contact with banking legislation, but I have seen more rotten practices among banks in New York City than you have. Regulations and penalties will not stop them if they want to resume speculation."[20] In August, the president was even more adamant when he wrote to Glass:

> As to underwriting of securities by banks, I am frankly wholly opposed. The provision in the Senate bill for a so-called safeguard through open market sales is not a safeguard. If you were not of such a trusting and unsuspicious nature, and if you had my experience with certain elements in certain places you would know that the old abuses would come back if underwriting were restored in any shape, manner or form.
>
> One other thought—two years ago you and I were agreed that the underwriting of securities never was and never should be a legitimate right or action on the part of commercial banks. I honestly think a great question of principle is involved and I cannot change my opinion, especially as it is based on a great many years of practical experience with these banking institutions which conducted such underwriting in the past.[21]

In the face of FDR's opposition, Glass dropped his proposal.

10

GLASS'S RECORD
AND LEGACY

Curb of bigness is indispensable to true Democracy & liberty....
Remember, the inevitable ineffectiveness of regulation.

—Louis D. Brandeis

Carter Glass was not a theorist. He did not spell out his economic
and political beliefs in books and articles. Glass was a practical politician who served as a congressman, Secretary of the Treasury, and
senator for over forty-three years. Like other men of action, Glass was
not entirely consistent. He had the nation's first securities disclosure
bill prepared in 1919 when he was Secretary of the Treasury. Later, as
a senator, he showed no interest in this topic when Congress considered the Securities Act of 1933. Glass drafted the Glass-Steagall Act of
1933 to prohibit banks and their affiliates from underwriting and dis-
tributing securities. Just two years later, he proposed legislation that
would have permitted banks to re-enter major areas of the securities
business.

Despite these and other inconsistencies, Glass's overall record—
his speeches, floor statements in the House and Senate, questions at
congressional hearings, private correspondence, and above all, his
actions—demonstrate that Glass held consistent core beliefs.

First, Glass generally opposed an activist federal government.
This was evidenced by his fierce hostility to the vast majority of New

Deal laws.

Second, Glass feared powerful financial interests. Therefore, he made exceptions to his usual opposition to government involvement in the case of laws designed to curb concentrated financial power.

Third, Glass favored a legislative approach that sought to curb financial power by fragmenting that power rather than by seeking to regulate it. Thus, he drafted the Federal Reserve Act of 1913 to create a number of regional reserve banks instead of a singular central bank. Later, he drafted the Glass-Steagall Act of 1933 to separate commercial and investment banking activities, rather than authorizing the Federal Reserve Board and the Comptroller of the Currency to regulate bank security affiliates. At times, Glass also pursued a fragmentation approach with respect to government. Following this logic in 1934, he succeeded in lodging jurisdiction over securities activities in a new specialized agency, the United States Securities and Exchange Commission, rather than in a large existing agency with other responsibilities, the Federal Trade Commission.

Glass did not construct his proposals from scratch. Instead, he used existing models and suggestions put forth by others. Glass based the regional reserve bank approach of the Federal Reserve Act on the existence of clearinghouses in major cities that facilitated transactions between banks in that region.[1] In drafting the Federal Reserve Act, Glass borrowed many technical provisions from the Aldrich Plan. Two decades before the Glass-Steagall Act separated commercial and investment banking, the Pujo subcommittee and Louis Brandeis had urged this very reform. Before Glass proposed creation of the SEC, the Roper Committee, Senator King, and the Twentieth Century Fund had called for the establishment of a specialized securities agency. However, while Glass did not originate these proposals, he was the person most responsible for getting them enacted into law.

Glass's major efforts in the financial area all had the same goal—preventing the flow of money from communities around the country to Wall Street to fund securities speculation. As an unknown congressman, Glass had been assigned the difficult task of designing reserve banking legislation and getting it enacted into law. Glass was extremely proud of his accomplishment, the Federal Reserve Act of 1913. The act created a unique geographically decentralized reserve banking system precisely in order to curtail the movement of funds from across the nation to northern financial markets. Much of Glass's work after 1913 was designed to preserve this decentralized system. Thus, one of Glass's main goals in the Glass-Steagall Act was to stop the use of the regional Federal Reserve Banks he helped create in the Federal Reserve Act to assist in directing money from their local communities to Wall Street. In 1934, Glass supported creation of the SEC in an attempt to keep the Federal Reserve System free from entanglement with securities markets. Glass opposed the Roosevelt Administration's 1935 banking legislation since he feared it would convert the decentralized Federal Reserve System into a central bank that inevitably would be controlled by northern financial interests.

Development of Glass's Beliefs

Glass's political and economic beliefs had their origin in his views regarding post–Civil War Virginia. Like most of his white southern contemporaries, Glass was an unabashed racist who saw Reconstruction and the Readjuster Party as unmitigated disasters. During the currency debates in the latter part of the nineteenth century, Glass developed a similar animosity toward another outside force, big city financial interests.

Glass's views regarding the federal government and Wall Street were reinforced by his government service during the Wilson Administration, where he was surrounded by other white southerners. Like Glass, they were raised in a region where, in Robert Wiebe's words, "Traditional hostilities toward national interference permeated the atmosphere."[2] President Wilson was from the South, as were his Secretary of the Treasury, William Gibbs McAdoo, and his chief economic adviser, Louis Brandeis. Democrats controlled both houses of Congress, and over half of the Democratic senators and over 40 percent of Democratic House members were from the South. Southerners served as Speaker of the House and Majority Leader in the Senate. Southerners were named as chairmen of twelve of the fourteen Senate committees and eleven of the thirteen House committees.

In 1912, Wilson had campaigned for the presidency against Republican President Taft and Progressive Party candidate Theodore Roosevelt. Roosevelt called for the New Nationalism, which meant greater federal regulation of big business and finance. Wilson, advised by Brandeis, advocated the New Freedom, which meant greater federal efforts to enhance competition. Brandeis wrote, "[Roosevelt's Progressive] Party does not fear commercial power, however great, if only methods for regulation are provided. We [the Democrats] believe that no methods of regulation ever have been or can be devised to remove the menace inherent in private monopoly and overweening commercial power."[3]

Once Wilson was in office, Glass was an enthusiastic supporter of Wilson's New Freedom programs, which reflected Glass's own inclinations. Thus, Glass authored the Federal Reserve Act, which provided for a number of regional reserve banks rather than one central bank and voted for Wilson's proposals to strengthen the antitrust laws.

There was a striking similarity in the backgrounds and views held by Glass and Brandeis. Both were born in the South just before the start of the Civil War (Brandeis in 1856 in Kentucky, Glass in 1858 in Virginia). Both grew up in the post–Civil War South, with its antipathy to interference from both the federal government and powerful northern interests. Both men made an exception to their opposition to federal government action in the case of laws aimed at curbing powerful financial interests. Thus, they both were involved in the development of the Federal Reserve Act, with its stress on geographic decentralization and public control of the banking system. In his 1913 book *Other People's Money and How the Bankers Use It,* Brandeis called for the separation of commercial and investment banking; Glass accomplished separation in 1933 in the Glass-Steagall Act. In his book, Brandeis also called for a securities disclosure law. In 1919, when Glass was Secretary of the Treasury, he had the nation's first securities disclosure bill prepared and introduced in Congress.

Franklin Roosevelt's election as president in 1932 presented Glass, Brandeis, and other southern progressives with a conundrum. Even before Roosevelt assumed office, Glass worried that he was likely to pursue policies providing for greatly increased federal authority. Some of FDR's early programs, such as the Securities Act, the Securities Exchange Act, and the Glass-Steagall Act, implemented New Freedom ideas, and therefore Glass supported them. But others, like the National Industrial Recovery Act and the Agricultural Adjustment Act, embodied the very kind of massive federal interference in the private sector that Glass feared. Many, if not most, of the old Wilsonian progressives, including Glass, broke with the New Deal.[4]

In particular, Glass called the National Industrial Recovery Act "arbitrary, senseless, and brutal," and "Hitlerism."[5] After Brandeis and his Supreme Court colleagues declared the act unconstitutional, Brandeis told Roosevelt's aides, "This is the end of this business of centralization.... I want you to go back and tell the President that we're not going to let this government centralize everything. It's come to an end."[6] More generally, Glass railed against the vast increase in federal power during the New Deal, stating that "the federal government [is] protruding its nose into all kinds of business," and predicting "the righteous failure of every damned project that these arbitrary little bureaucrats are vainly endeavoring to put in effect."[7]

Similarly, Brandeis stated: "The United States should go back to the federation idea, letting each state evolve a policy and develop itself. There are enough good men in Alabama, for example, to make

Alabama a good state. But the tendency is to put responsibility upon the federal Government."[8]

Popularity of the New Nationalism Approach

Since World War II, the nation generally has followed the New Nationalism approach of imposing greater regulation on the financial sector, rather than the New Freedom approach of fragmenting concentrated financial power. Most notably, in 1999 Congress enacted the Gramm-Leach-Bliley Act, which repealed the Glass-Steagall Act's provisions that prohibited banking organizations from owning securities firms. As a result, today large universal banking organizations engage in all aspects of the securities business. Congress also has enacted a long series of financial laws imposing new regulatory requirements on the financial sector.[9] As part of this legislation Congress has created a large number of new regulatory agencies. In 1912 the only federal financial regulator was the Comptroller of the Currency, who oversaw national banks. Today there are more than a dozen federal agencies and quasi-agencies that regulate the financial sector.[10]

This New Nationalism approach reached a new peak when Congress responded to the 2008 financial crisis by enacting the Dodd-Frank Wall Street Reform and Consumer Protection Act of 2010. The act runs 848 pages and directs regulators to adopt 243 new rules, to undertake sixty-seven major studies, and to prepare twenty-two reports. Many rules that have been adopted run for dozens of pages. The so-called Volcker Rule dealing with proprietary trading by banks is seventy-one pages long and has an 850 page preface. The Act also created the Financial Stability Oversight Council, a group of ten financial regulatory agencies that has the authority to determine that a particular nonbank financial institution poses a threat to the stability of the financial system and therefore should be made subject to heightened prudential requirements.

Glass's Legacy

Despite increased use of the New Nationalism regulatory approach exemplified by the Dodd-Frank Act, Glass's approach of fragmenting financial power still remains the cornerstone of the American financial system. The financial laws that form the basis of our financial system—the Federal Reserve Act, the Securities Exchange Act, and the Glass-Steagall Act—continue to function largely as Glass intended:

> Glass drafted the Federal Reserve Act of 1913 to create a unique geographically decentralized reserve banking system. Beginning with the Banking Act of 1935 some authority has been shifted from regional reserve banks to the Federal Reserve Board in Washington, DC. However, the system still functions within the decentralized structure designed by Glass. Today, there are proposals to further increase the authority of the board (for example, to give it responsibility to name the heads of the regional banks), but no one is proposing to do away with Glass's core concept of geographic decentralization.[11]

> In 1934, as Glass proposed, the SEC was created as a stand-alone independent agency, rather than as part of a larger governmental body, the approach favored by New Dealers. Shortly after the SEC was created, there was a call for "unifying ... governmental agencies which regulate the operations of security capitalism ... into a Federal Finance system which would exercise all the powers now performed by these separate agencies."[12] Similar proposals have been put forth over the ensuing years. None have been enacted. Thus, the SEC remains a stand-alone federal agency devoted solely to the regulation of securities activities, just as Glass intended.

In 1999, the Glass-Steagall Act was amended to permit commercial banks to affiliate with securities firms, thus undoing one of the act's major reforms. However, other provisions, including those limiting bank lending for securities speculation (Glass's primary objective), providing for federal insurance of bank deposits, prohibiting direct bank involvement in securities activities, and barring securities firms from taking deposits, remain in place.

It is not surprising that over the decades these most important financial laws have been amended to meet new conditions and to reflect new theories. What is surprising is how much of the basic regulatory superstructure created by Glass is still in place.

Today, there is widespread belief that the Dodd-Frank Act has not lessened the chances of a major financial crisis. Neil Barofsky, the former Special Inspector General of the Treasury, has warned, "We had a system that was broken ... and the fundamentals within that system haven't changed." "'The question is not if" the United States faces another financial disaster, he warned, "'it's when.'" David Primo, Professor of Political Science and Business Administration at the University of Rochester, predicted, "Dodd-Frank will do nothing to prevent another financial crisis."[13]

There is also concern that we now have a handful of giant banks and that a crisis threatening just one of them will cause a catastrophe. Thomas Hoenig, former vice chairman of the Federal Deposit Insurance Corporation, has noted that the United States now has a financial industry "that is far more concentrated, complex, and government dependent than at any time in recent history. In 1990, for example, the five largest U.S. financial holding companies controlled only 20 percent of total industry assets. Today that number is 55 percent and will likely increase. Ironically, these events also have left the U.S. economy increasingly vulnerable to industry mistakes."[14]

These concerns have led to proposals to impose new controls along the lines of Glass's fragmentation approach to financial regulation. A bi-partisan group of senators has introduced legislation to restore the Glass-Steagall Act's provisions separating banks and securities firms. Another proposal would go a step further and require the separation of banks from both securities firms and asset managers. Two Democratic senators have proposed legislative limits on the size of banks. Others have suggested imposing similar size limits on securities firms. Another idea is to create a new institution, "The Sentinel," whose sole responsibility would be to assess and report annually on the efficacy of financial laws and regulations.[15]

Glass's legacy can be found not only in the laws that underlie the American financial system but also in current-day proposals to improve the functioning of that system.

Glass's record demonstrates the characteristics that a public leader needs in order to obtain enactment of meaningful financial reform legislation.

First, Glass excelled at anticipating and planning for future legislation. From the moment he was appointed to the House Banking Committee in 1903, Glass spent his time diligently studying banking issues. Therefore, when the Democrats took control of Congress in 1912, Glass was able to formulate a reserve banking bill and then present it to President-elect Wilson. The final result was the Federal Reserve Act, often described as the most important financial law in U.S. history. In the 1920s, Glass became concerned with the use of the reserve banking system to fuel stock market speculation. He began developing remedial legislation after the 1929 crash and was able to present a reform bill, passed by the Senate, to President-elect Franklin Roosevelt. The result was the Glass-Steagall Act, which Roosevelt called "the second most important banking legislation in the history of our country."

Second, Glass showed great skill in shepherding complicated and controversial financial laws through Congress. Glass's ability to understand complex issues and explain them to others, his focus on what mattered, his readiness to take on both powerful politicians and well-heeled financial interests, his willingness to compromise when necessary, and, above all, his determination and "pluck" in pursuing his principal objectives were extraordinary.

Third, Glass demonstrated remarkable independence and steadfastness. His faults did not include an overriding desire to be popular. Glass said, "I've acted in the way I felt I should and then let the people decide for themselves if they approved of my actions. I have never considered what effect my actions would have upon the continuance of my public career. I have done what I thought was best for the country."[16] Glass's long-time Senate colleague, Republican senator Norbeck of South Dakota, put it well in a letter to a constituent: "Senator Glass's banking creed is his religion,—and while he may write you a nice letter, he will not yield an inch or a fraction of an inch,—at least this is my view after close association with him for over twelve years."[17]

Today's and tomorrow's policy makers can improve and build upon the American financial system that Glass did so much to create. In order to be successful policy makers, they will need to emulate Glass's personal approach to the legislative process, namely his diligence, hard work, independent thinking, and "pluck."

INTRODUCTION NOTES

1. James T. Patterson, *Congressional Conservatism and the New Deal: The Growth of the Conservative Coalition in Congress, 1933–1939* (Lexington, KY: University of Kentucky Press, 1967, rpt., Westport, CT: Greenwood Press, 1981), 20, n.1.
2. Rixey Smith and Norman Beasley, *Carter Glass: A Biography* (New York: Longmans, Green, 1939); and James E. Palmer, Jr., *Carter Glass: Unreconstructed Rebel* (Roanoke, VA: Institute of American Biography, 1938).
3. Otis L, Graham, Jr., *An Encore for Reform: The Old Progressives and the New Deal* (London: Oxford University Press, 1967), 89; "Congress Acts in Unison; Orders Dial Phones Ousted," *New York American,* May 23, 1930; Patterson, *Congressional Conservatism,* 21; Glass to L. W. Douglas, November 26, 1935, Box 341, Carter Glass Manuscripts, University of Virginia. [hereafter cited as Glass MSS]; and Smith and Beasley, *Carter Glass,* 256.

CHAPTER 1 NOTES

1. Glass's background is discussed in Harry Edward Poindexter, "From Copy Desk to Congress: The Pre-Congressional Career of Carter Glass" (doctoral thesis, University of Virginia, 1966); Smith and Beasley, *Carter Glass,* 1–60; Palmer, *Carter Glass,* 11–50; and Roger Lowenstein, *America's Bank: The Epic Struggle to Create the Federal Reserve* (New York: Penguin, 2015), 17–18.
2. Smith and Beasley, *Carter Glass,* 30.
3. Poindexter, "From Copy Desk to Congress," 99.
4. Glass Remarks at Monticello, July 4, 1936, Box 380, Glass MSS.
5. Palmer, *Carter Glass,* 17.
6. Smith and Beasley, *Carter Glass,* 2–3.
7. Ibid, 13.
8. Ibid, 497.

9. Ibid, 30–31.
10. Glass to A. G. Kelly, November 14, 1935, Box 341, Glass MSS.
11. *Lynchburg News*, March 15, 1889.
12. Smith and Beasley, *Carter Glass*, 37.
13. Poindexter, "From Copy Desk to Congress," 125–26.
14. Ibid, 128.
15. *Lynchburg News*, April 28, 1893.
16. Ibid, May 9, 1893.
17. Ibid, March 21, 1894.
18. Poindexter, "From Copy Desk to Congress," 137.
19. Palmer, *Carter Glass*, 43–44.
20. Poindexter, "From Copy Desk to Congress," 473–74; and Allan A. Michie and Frank Ryhlick, *Dixie Demagogues* (New York: Vanguard, 1939), 177, 178.
21. Palmer, *Carter Glass*, 47.

CHAPTER 2 NOTES

1. Horace Samuel Merrill and Marion Galbraith Merrill, *The Republican Command 1897–1913* (Lexington, KY: University Press of Kentucky, 1971), 9, 4–5.
2. Palmer, *Carter Glass*, 54.
3. Jeffrey M. Lacker, "A Look Back at the History of the Federal Reserve," speech, Chrisopher Newport University, Newport News, VA, August 29, 2013.
4. Elmus Wicker, *The Great Debate on Banking Reform: Nelson Aldrich and the Origins of the Fed* (Columbus: Ohio State University Press, 2005), 22–38.
5. Lacker, "A Look Back."
6. Frederick Lewis Allen, *The Lords of Creation* (New York: Harper & Brothers, 1935), 197.
7. Paul M. Warburg, "Defects and Needs of Our Banking System," *New York Times Annual Financial Review*, January 6, 1907, 14.

8. Roger Lowenstein, *America's Bank*, 38, 33.
9. Jacob Schiff, speech, New York Chamber of Commerce, January 4, 1906, *Forty-Eighth Annual Report of the New York Chamber of Commerce*, Pt 1 (New York: Press of the New York Chamber of Commerce, 1906), 110–11.
10. Farley, *Wall Street Wars*, 4; and Ron Chernow, *The House of Morgan: An American Banking Dynasty and the Rise of Modern Finance* (New York: Grove, 1990), 122.
11. Robert F. Bruner and Sean D. Carr, *The Panic of 1907: Lessons Learned From the Market's Perfect Storm* (Hoboken, NJ: John Wiley, 2007), 67.
12. Allen, *Lords of Creation*, 119.
13. Chernow, *House of Morgan*, 124.
14. Allen, *Lords of Creation*, 130.
15. Peter Conti-Brown, *The Power and Independence of the Federal Reserve* (Princeton: Princeton University Press, 2016), 158.
16. Nathaniel Wright Stephenson, *Nelson W. Aldrich: A Leader in American Politics* (New York: Scribner's, 1930), 384.
17. Wicker, *Great Debate*, 3.
18. *Congressional Record* 42 (Pt. 8), 7068–69 (May 27, 1908).
19. Wicker, *Great Debate*, 50.
20. Lowenstein, *America's Bank*, 88.
21. Merrill, *Republican Command*, 7–8.
22. Conti-Brown, *Power and Independence*, 19.
23. Lowenstein, *America's Bank*, 134–37.
24. Stephenson, *Nelson W. Aldrich*, 404; Arthur S. Link, *Wilson: The New Freedom* (Princeton, Princeton University Press, 1956), 201; and Gabriel Kolko, *The Triumph of Conservatism: A Reinterpretation of American History, 1910–1916* (New York: Free Press, 1963), 189.

CHAPTER 3 NOTES

1. George Wheeler, *Pierpont Morgan and Friends: The Anatomy of a Myth* (Englewood Cliffs, NJ: Prentice-Hall, 1973), 292–93.

2. Jean Strouse, *Morgan: American Financier* (New York: Random House, 1999, rpt., New York, HarpersCollins, 2000), 659.

3. Glass later wrote that Pujo had offered him the choice of chairing either subcommittee and that he had chosen the subcommittee that was to formulate reserve banking legislation. Glass to George W. Norris, September 17, 1920, Box 24, Glass MSS.

4. Henry F. Pringle, *Big Frogs* (New York: Macy-Masius, 1928), 148, 149.

5. *Report of the Committee Appointed Pursuant to House Resolutions 429 and 504 to Investigate the Concentration of Control of Money and Credit*, 62d Cong., 3d sess., 129 and 133 (1913).

6. Ibid, 162–73.

7. The latter recommendation was made in response to the attempts by National City Bank and other large banks to create securities affiliates. The report stated, "national banks should not be permitted to become inseparably tied together with security holding companies ... [that] have unlimited powers to buy and sell and speculate in stocks.... It is unsafe for banks to be united with them. ... The temptation would be great at times to use the bank's funds to finance the speculative operations of the holding company....The mistakes or misfortunes of the latter are too likely to react upon the former." Ibid, 151, 155.

8. Kolko, *Triumph of Conservatism*, 220.

9. Louis D. Brandeis, *Other People's Money and How the Bankers Use It* (New York: Frederick A. Stokes, 1913); and Melvin I. Urofsky, *Louis D. Brandeis: A Life* (New York: Pantheon, 2009), 381.

10. Brandeis, *Other People's Money,* 5–6, 26–27, and 92–108. Brandeis also endorsed specific reforms called for by the Pujo subcommittee's report, including separating commercial and investment banking and requiring corporate issuers of securities to provide disclosures to investors.

11. Carter Glass, *An Adventure in Constructive Finance* (Garden City, NY: Doubleday, 1927), 68; Glass to George W. Norris, September 17, 1920, Box 24, Glass MSS; and Joseph Stagg Lawrence, *Wall Street and Washington* (Princeton: Princeton University Press, 1929), 371.

12. John Milton Cooper, Jr., *Woodrow Wilson: A Biography* (New York: Alfred A. Knopf, 2009), 220.

13. Glass, *Adventure,* 70.

14. Henry Parker Willis, *The Federal Reserve System: Legislation, Organization and Operation* (New York: Ronald Press, 1923), 133–34.

15. Glass to Wilson, November 7, 1912, Box 6, Glass MSS.

16. Wilson to Glass, November 14, 1912, reprinted in Glass, *Adventure,* 75.

17. Pujo to Glass, November 12, 1912, Box 1, Henry Parker Willis Manuscripts, Columbia University [hereafter cited as Willis MSS]; and Glass to Willis, December 3, 1912, Boxes 25 and 26, Glass MSS.

18. Glass to Edna E. Gaines, July 21, 1927, Box 252; and Glass to R. C. Leffingwell, July 15, 1927, Box 5, Glass MSS.

19. Glass to Willis, December 29, 1912; and Glass to Willis, January 3, 1913, Box 1, Willis MSS.

20. John Milton Cooper, Jr., *The Warrior and the Priest: Woodrow Wilson and Theodore Roosevelt* (Cambridge, MA: Belknap, 1983), 233.

21. Glass to Wilson, December 29, 1912, Box 6, Glass MSS.

22. Kolko, *Triumph of Conservatism,* 225–26.

23. Glass, *Adventure,* 91–92.

24. Glass to Wilson, May 15, 1913, Box 17, Glass MSS.

25. Glass to A. B. Hepburn, May 30, 1913, Box 38, Glass MSS: and Glass, *Adventure*, 108.

26. Glass to George M. Reynolds, June 9, 1913, Box 17, Glass MSS.

27. Link, *Wilson*, 211–12.

28. Ibid, 212.

29. Glass to Wilson, June 18, 1913, Box 8, Glass MSS.

30. Link, *Wilson*, 214.

31. William G. McAdoo, *Crowded Years: The Reminiscences of William G. McAdoo* (Boston: Houghton Mifflin, 1931), 224–25.

32. *New York Times*, June 21, 1913; and Link, *Wilson*, 225.

33. Link, *Wilson*, 215–16.

34. McAdoo, *Crowded Years*, 226.

35. Glass, *Adventure*, 116.

36. Willis, *Federal Reserve System*, 361.

37. John Douglas Lyle, "The Role of Carter Glass in the Formulation and Enactment of the Federal Reserve Act" (master's thesis, University of South Carolina, 1968), 49–50.

38. Bryan to Glass, August 22, 1913, Box 17, Glass MSS.

39. McAdoo to Glass, September 20, 1913, reprinted in Palmer, *Carter Glass*, 118.

40. Glass to Bryan, September 25, 1913, Box 17, Glass MSS.

41. McAdoo, *Crowded Years*, 249.

42. Carter Glass, "The Opposition to the Federal Reserve Bank Bill," *Proceedings of the Academy of Political Science in the City of New York*, 4, no. 1 (October 1913), 19.

43. McAdoo, *Crowded Years*, 252–53.

44. Lyle, "Role of Carter Glass," 80.

45. Link, *Wilson*, 238.

46. Warburg to Glass, December 23, 1913, Box 17, Glass MSS.

47. Wilson to Glass, December 25, 1913, reprinted in Palmer, *Carter Glass*, 118.

48. "The Currency Bill," *Elmira Star-Gazette*, February 27, 1914; and Allen, *Lords of Creation*, 199.

49. The arguments of the various parties are discussed in Lowenstein, *America's Bank*, 266–70.

50. Glass, *Adventure*, 247–48; and Willis, *Federal Reserve System*, 523.

51. Johnson, *Winthrop W. Aldrich*, 33; and Wicker, *Great Debate*, 54.

52. Allen, *Lords of Creation*, 199; and Alexander Dana Noyes, *The Market Place: Reminiscences of a Financial Editor* (Boston: Little Brown, 138), 242.

53. Conti-Brown, *Power and Independence*, 126.

54. Glass, *Adventure*, 173–74.

55. Stephenson, *Nelson W. Aldrich*, 414.

56. Thomas W. Lamont, *Henry P. Davison: The Record of a Useful Life* (New York: Harper & Brothers, 1933), 104.

57. Glass to R. D. Haislip, November 28, 1919, Box 4, Glass MSS.

58. James Livingston, *Origins of the Federal Reserve System: Money, Class, and Corporate Capitalism, 1890–1913* (Ithaca, NY: Cornell University Press, 1986), 215.

59. George W. Edwards, *The Evolution of Finance Capitalism* (London: Longmans, Green, 1938), 199; and Noyes, *Market Place*, 244.

60. Will Rogers, "Rogers Becomes Cabinet Picker," *Boston Globe*, January 29, 1933.

CHAPTER 4 NOTES

1. Glass to John Stewart Bryan, November 3, 1921, cited in Chester B. Goolrick, Jr., "Carter Glass: Wilson's Apostle" (master's thesis, University of Virginia, 1950), 27.

2. Wilson to Glass, June 15, 1916, Box 8, Glass MSS.

3. "Glass for Reserve Board," *Washington Post*, November 30, 1918.

4. Julia C. Ott, *When Wall Street Met Main Street: The Quest for an Investors' Democracy* (Cambridge, MA: Harvard University Press, 2011), 2.

5. Smith and Beasley, *Carter Glass,* 173.

6. *Federal Reserve Bulletin, January 1919* ((Washington, D.C.: U.S. Government Printing Office, 1919), 18.

7. John Douglas Lyle, "The United States Senate Career of Carter Glass, 1920–1933" (doctoral thesis, University of South Carolina, 1974), 21–24; and letter from Charles S. Hamlin, Chairman, Capital Issue Committee, to Glass, October 28, 1919, Box 141, Glass MSS.

8. Draft of Federal Stock Publicity Act, February 7, 1919, Box 144, Glass MSS; and H.R. 15922, 65th Cong., 3d sess., February 13, 1919.

9. Smith and Beasley, *Carter Glass,* 159–60.

10. Ibid, 179–80.

11. Letter from Wilson to Glass, November 17, 1919, Box 8, Glass MSS.

12. Goolrick, "Carter Glass," 34.

13. Ibid.

14. Lyle, "Senate Career of Carter Glass," 54–55.

15. Glass to John Skelton Williams, June 17, 1921, Box 218, Glass MSS.

16. Glass to John R. Hutcheson, July 26, 1923, Box 342, Glass MSS.

17. Glass to George D. Ellis, November 8, 1923, Box 226, Glass MSS.

18. Lawrence, *Wall Street and Washington,* 371.

19. Robert Sobel, *The Great Bull Market: Wall Street in the 1920s* (New York: W. W. Norton, 1968), 74.

20. John Kenneth Galbraith, *The Great Crash 1929* (Boston: Houghton Mifflin, 1954), 22.

21. Ibid.

22. Ibid, 32.

23. Glass to Norman C. Finninger, January 7, 1928, Box 352; and Glass to Lloyd R. Freeman, March 5, 1928, Box 252, Glass MSS.

24. Carter Glass, "The Federal Reserve Act Grossly Misused," *The American Review of Reviews,* 78 (September 1928), 257–58.

25. Glass to Platt, April 26, 1928, Box 46, Glass MSS.
26. Sobel, *Great Bull Market,* 115–16.
27. Galbraith, *Great Crash 1929,* 33.
28. Ibid, 34.
29. Ibid, 37–38
30. Lyle, "United States Senate Career of Carter Glass," 147–48.
31. Glass letter to the editor, "Stock Gambling," *New York Times,* August 21, 1929.
32. Lyle, "United States Senate Career of Carter Glass," 151–52.
33. "An Impossible Definition," *Wall Street Journal,* February 16, 1929.
34. "As Senators See Stock Speculation," *New York Herald,* February 13, 1929.
35. Lawrence, *Wall Street and Washington,* v.
36. Ibid, v, vi, and vii.
37. Glass letter to the *Philadelphia Record,* October 31, 1929.
38. Galbraith, *Great Crash 1929,* 144.

CHAPTER 5 NOTES

1. *Congressional Record,* 72, 8335 (May 5, 1930).
2. Helen M. Burns, *The American Banking Community and New Deal Banking Reforms 1933–1935* (Westport, CT: Greenwood Press, 1974), 17.
3. H. Parker Willis and John M. Chapman, *The Banking Situation: American Post-War Problems and Developments* (New York: Columbia University Press, 1934), 57–58.
4. The development of bank security affiliates is set forth in Edwin J. Perkins, "The Divorce of Commercial and Investment Banking: A History," *Banking Law Journal,* 88, no. 6 (June 1971), 486–97. The leading study of security affiliates is W. Nelson Peach, *The Securities Affiliates of National Banks* (Baltimore: Johns Hopkins Press, 1941.)

5. Henry Parker Willis, "Reforms Due in Investment Banking—and in Bank Relations to Affiliates," *The Annalist*, 35, no. 887 (January 17, 1930), 114–44.
6. Willis and Chapman, *Banking Situation*, 68.
7. S. 4723, 71st Cong., 2d sess., *Congressional Record* 72, 10,973 (June 17, 1930).
8. Willis and Chapman, *Banking Situation*, 65.
9. The bill did not provide for regulation of securities affiliates of state-chartered banks that were not members of the Federal Reserve System because Glass and others believed there was no basis for federal regulation of purely state institutions.
10. *Operation of the National and Federal Reserve Banking Systems: Hearings Pursuant to Senate Resolution 71 Before a Subcommittee of the Senate Committee on Banking and Currency*, 71st Cong., 3d sess. (1931). [hereafter *1931 Hearings*]
11. Ibid, 41.
12. "Bank's Depositors Ask Governor's Aid," *New York Times*, December 25, 1930, 25.
13. *1931 Hearings*, 22, 116, 193–94, 212–13, 237, 258, 266, 271, 307, and 317.
14. Ibid, J. W. Pole testimony, 2–30; George L. Harrison testimony, 31–106; Arthur C. Miller testimony, 123–63; and Arthur C. Miller views of affiliates, 148.
15. Ibid, 271–83.
16. *1931 Hearings*, Pt. 7, 1000.
17. Ibid, 1058.
18. Ibid, 1063–64.
19. Ibid, 1068.
20. Susan Easterbrook Kennedy, *The Banking Crisis of 1933* (Lexington, KY: University Press of Kentucky, 1973), 19.

21. Joan Hoff Wilson, *Herbert Hoover: Forgotten Progressive* (New York: HarperCollins, 1975, rpt., Long Grove, IL: Waveland Press, 1992), 137; and Marcus Nadler and Jules L. Bogen, *The Banking Crisis: The End of an Epoch* (New York: Dodd Mead, 1933, rpt., New York: Arno, 1980), 49.

22. Kennedy, *Banking Crisis*, 25.

23. Willis and Chapman, *Banking Situation*, 84.

24. Nadler and Bogen, *Banking Crisis*, 51; and Willis and Chapman, *Banking Situation*, 90.

25. Nadler and Bogen, *Banking Crisis*, 52.

26. S. 3215, 72d Cong., 1st sess., *Congressional Record* 75, 2403 (January 21, 1932).

27. Lyle, "United States Senate Career of Carter Glass," 214–18.

28. Glass to John M. Miller, Jr., May 13, 1932, Box 311, Glass MSS; and Willis and Chapman, *Banking Situation*, 68–69.

29. Glass to Winthrop A. Mandell, December 5, 1931, Boxes 302 and 303; and Glass to E. A. Purdy, December 23, 1931, Boxes 302 and 303, Glass MSS.

30. Note 11 *supra*.

31. Willis to Glass, March 10, 1930, Box 1, Willis MSS.

32. Glass to F. A. Delano, February 16, 1923, Box 352; and Glass to George L. Harrison, March 22, 1933, Box 31, Glass MSS.

33. Glass to C. S. Hamlin, April 6, 1931, Boxes 278 and 279, Glass MSS.

34. C. S. Hamlin to Glass, September 29, 1932, Box 299, Glass MSS.

35. "Wall Street Faces Inquiry By Congress," *New York Times*, September 13, 1931.

36. Raymond Moley, *The First New Deal* (New York: Harcourt, Brace & World, 1966), 317.

37. "To Offer Glass Bill With Few Changes: Senate Banking Committee Will Report the Measure Early Next Week," *New York Times*, January 23, 1932, 24; and Nadler and Bogen, *Banking Crisis*, 53.

38. *Congressional Record*, 75, 2999 (February 1, 1932).

39. S. 4115, 72d Cong., 2d sess. (March 14, 1932); and *Operation of the National and Federal Reserve Banking Systems: Hearings on S. 4115 Before the Senate Committee on Banking and Currency*, 72d Cong., 1st sess. (1932). [hereafter *1932 Hearings*]

40. *1932 Hearings*, 357; and Glass to Meyer, March 21, 1932, Box 5, Glass MSS.

41. S. 4412, 72d Cong., 2d sess., *Congressional Record* 75, 8350 (January 30, 1932).

42. Senate Report No. 584, 72d Cong., 1st sess., 9 (1932).

43. *Congressional Record*, 75, 9887 (May 10, 1932).

44. Perkins, "Divorce of Commercial and Investment Banking," 517; and letter from Irving Dillard to Glass, March 10, 1933, enclosing editorial from *St. Louis Post Dispatch* of March 10, 1933, alleging that the affiliate system was "always illegal," Box 419, Glass MSS.

45. Smith and Beasley, *Carter Glass*, 308–9.

46. Burns, *American Banking Community*, 23.

47. Ibid, 23–24.

48. Carter Glass, Radio Speech, "The Facts About the Fiscal Policy of Our Government During the Past Few Years," November 1, 1932, reprinted in Smith and Beasley, *Carter Glass*, 473–75.

49. Ibid, 495.

50. *Washington Herald*, November 3, 1932, Box 9, Glass MSS; *Washington Evening Star*, January 4, 1933, Box 8, Glass MSS; Charles S. McCain to Glass, November 25, 1932, Box 311, Glass MSS; and Roosevelt to Glass, November 2, 1932, Boxes 6 and 298, Glass MSS.

51. Perkins, "Divorce of Commercial and Investment Banking," 519.

52. Lyle, "United States Senate Career of Carter Glass," 293.

53. Kennedy, *Banking Crisis*, 73.

CHAPTER 6 NOTES

1. Kennedy, *Banking Crisis*, 68.

2. Ibid, 70.
3. Nadler and Bogen, *Banking Crisis,* 146.
4. Samuel I. Rosenman, ed., *The Public Papers and Addresses of Franklin D. Roosevelt* (New York: Macmillan, 1941), vol. 2, 11–15.
5. Glass to R. G. Leffingwell, July 12, 1933, Box 147, Glass MSS.
6. Anthony J. Badger, *FDR: The First Hundred Days* (New York: Hill and Wang, 2008), 41.
7. *Congressional Record,* 77, 58 (March 9, 1933); and Farley, *Wall Street Wars,* 52.
8. The history of government insurance of bank deposits is set forth in Carter H. Golembe, "The Deposit Insurance Legislation of 1933: An Examination of Its Antecedents and Its Purposes," *Political Science Quarterly,* 75, no. 2 (June, 1960), 181–200.
9. Ibid, 189.
10. *To Provide a Guarantee Fund for Depositors in Banks: Hearings on H.R. 11362 Before the Subcommittee of the House Committee on Banking and Currency,* 72d Cong., 1st sess. (1932), 117.
11. Michael Perino, *The Hellhound of Wall Street: How Ferdinand Pecora's Investigation of the Great Crash Forever Changed American Finance* (New York: Penguin, 2010), 291.
12. Alfred Cash Koeniger, "'Unreconstructed Rebel': The Political Thought and Senate Career of Carter Glass, 1929–1936" (doctoral thesis, Vanderbilt University, 1980), 98–99.
13. Kennedy, *Banking Crisis,* 214.
14. Perino, *Hellhound of Wall Street,* 62.
15. Kennedy, *Banking Crisis,* 111.
16. Ibid, 114.
17. Perino, *Hellhound of Wall Street,* 155.
18. Alfred Cash Koeniger, "Carter Glass and the New Deal: From the Presidential Campaign of 1932 Through the Hundred Days Session of Congress" (master's thesis, Vanderbilt University, 1974), 75, n. 25.
19. Perino, *Hellhound of Wall Street,* 209.

20. Ibid, 210.
21. "Banking Reform Drafted," *New York Times*, April 8, 1933, 1.
22. *Congressional Record*, 77, 58 (March 9, 1933).
23. Kennedy, *Banking Crisis*, 212.
24. James Gerald Smith, "Banking and the Stock Market," in *Facing the Facts: an Economic Diagnosis*, ed. J. G. Smith (New York: G. P. Putnam's Sons, 1932), 153–85.
25. Perkins, "Divorce of Commercial and Investment Banking," 523.
26. Willis and Chapman, *Banking Situation*, 69.
27. Moley, *First New Deal*, 319.
28. Glass to R. B. Gunn, March 3, 1933, Box 6, Glass MSS; and Koeniger, "'Unreconstructed Rebel,'" 99.
29. Willis and Chapman, *Banking Situation*, 100.
30. "Roosevelt Hails Goal," *New York Times*, June 17, 1933, 1.
31. J. George Frederick, *A Primer of New Deal Economics* (New York: Business Bourse, 1933), 126; Roger W. Babson, *Washington and the Revolutionists* (New York: Harper & Brothers, 1934), 10–11; and Moley, *First New Deal*, 320.
32. James P. Warburg, *The Money Muddle* (New York: Alfred A. Knopf, 1934), 128; Samuel B. Pettengill, *Smoke Screen* (New York: Southern Publishers, 1940), 1–2, 80; John T. Flynn, "Other People's Money," *New Republic*, 75, 181, June 28, 1933; and John T. Flynn, *The Decline of the American Republic* (New York: Devin-Adair, 1955), 47.
33. Edwards, *Evolution of Finance Capitalism*, 296.

CHAPTER 7 NOTES

1. Otis L. Graham, Jr., *An Encore for Reform: The Old Progressives and the New Deal* (London: Oxford University Press, 1967), 27; and Frank Freidel, *F.D.R. and the South* (Baton Rouge: Louisiana State University Press, 1965), 24.
2. "Bills Must be Paid, Carter Glass Says," *New York Times,* July 28, 1930.
3. "Carter Glass on the Whisperers," *New York World,* September 29, 1928.
4. Glass to George H. Moses, November 14, 1932, Box 299; and Glass to R. L. Ailworth, November 11, 1932, Box 1, Glass MSS.
5. Smith and Beasley, *Carter Glass,* 337–38.
6. Glass to Willis, April 15, 1933, Box 382, Glass MSS.
7. Koeniger, "Unreconstructed Rebel," 142.
8. *Congressional Record,* 77, 73d Cong., 1st sess., April 27, 1933, 2461.
9. Koeniger, "Unreconstructed Rebel," 193.
10. Glass to James M. Beck, October 30, 1933, Boxes 308 and 309, Glass MSS.
11. Smith and Beasley, *Carter Glass,* 364.
12. Ibid, 361.
13. Glass to J. H. Carter, November 10, 1937, Box 380; Glass to Eli B. Manning, October 19, 1938, Box 383; and Glass to E. D. Bransome, February 25, 1939, Box 362, Glass MSS.

14. Glass to R. G. Leffingwell, July 12, 1933, Box 147; Glass to C. D. Moffitt, October 7, 1933, Box 312; Glass to William G. McAdoo, November 23, 1933, Box 13; Glass to H. D. Gould, January 8, 1935, Box 337; Glass to T. Norman Jones, Jr., February 20, 1935, Box 345; Glass to B. L. Peebles, April 8, 1935, Box 336; Glass to William F. H. Koelsch, May 20, 1935, Box 334; Glass to Percy Foster Hall, May 10, 1938, Box 362; and Glass to R. H. Barksdale, September 1, 1938, Box 383, Glass MSS.

15. Glass to Richard O'Laughlin, January 4, 1935, Box 331; Glass to Millard E. Tydings, October 9, 1936, Box 380; and Glass to J. Ernest Stack, August 31, 1937, Box 380, Glass MSS.

16. Glass to Millard E. Tydings, November 10, 1938, Box 383; Glass to J. F. Wieder, November 29, 1938, Box 383, Glass MSS; "Glass Won Fame in Finance Field," *New York Times*, May 29, 1946, 23: and "A Senator's Comment on Recognition," *Manchester Guardian*, November 19, 1933.

17. Patterson, *Congressional Conservatism*, 80–81.

18. Joseph Alsop and Turner Catledge, *The 168 Days* (Garden City, NY: Doubleday, 1938), 71; and Glass to Harry F. Byrd, May 17, 1937, Box 345, Glass MSS.

19. Carter Glass, "Constitutional Immorality," radio address, March 29, 1937, reprinted in Smith and Beasley, *Carter Glass*, 496, 510.

20. George Wolfskill and John A. Hudson, *All But the People: Franklin D. Roosevelt and His Critics, 1933–39* (London: Macmillan, 1969), 262.

21. Glass was not up for re-election in 1938.

22. Charles Peters, *Five Days in Philadelphia: The Amazing "We Want Willkie" Convention of 1940 and How It Freed FDR to Save the Western World* (New York: PublicAffairs, 2005), 138.

23. Ibid, 143–44.

24. *Congressional Record*, 77, 73d Cong., 1st sess., April 27, 1933, 2462.

25. Glass Remarks at Monticello, July 4, 1936, Box 380, Glass MSS; "President Points to 'Spirit of Youth' as Aid to Freedom," *New York Times*, July 5, 1936, 1; and Palmer, *Carter Glass*, 288.
26. Palmer, *Carter Glass*, 256; and Goolrick, "Carter Glass," 132
27. Palmer, *Carter Glass*, 257; Patterson, *Congressional Conservatism*, 19; and Freidel, *F.D.R. and the South*, 78.
28. Roosevelt's letter of December 12, 1933 to Glass is reprinted in Palmer, *Carter Glass*, 267. Glass's response to Roosevelt of December 15, 1933, is in Box 6, Glass MSS; Freidel, *F.D.R. and the South*, 78; and Glass to Carter Miller, October 2, 1935, Box 341, Glass MSS.
29. "Virginia Prospers: Roosevelt Strong," *New York Times*, December 4, 1935, 6; and Michie and Rhylic, *Dixie Demagogues*, 178–79.
30. Glass to Rixey Smith, November 21, 1938, Box 383, Glass MSS.
31. Glass to Julius Glass, October 6, 1936, Box 380, Glass MSS.
32. Glass to John S. Harris, September 15, 1939, Box 383: Glass to R. B. Stephenson, September 16, 1939, Box 383; Glass to W. H. Schwarzschild, Jr., May 14, 1940, Box 384, Glass MSS; and "To Fight Any Appropriation Cut," *New York Times*, March 17, 1941, 6.
33. Susan Dunn, *Roosevelt's Purge: How FDR Sought to Change the Democratic Party* (Cambridge, MA: Belknap Press, 2010), 219.
34. Glass to Roosevelt, March 2, 1941, Box 268, Glass MSS.
35. William E. Leuchtenburg, *The White House Looks South: Franklin D. Roosevelt, Harry S. Truman, Lyndon B. Johnson* (Baton Rouge: Louisiana State University Press, 2005), n. 38, 459–60.

CHAPTER 8 NOTES

1. *Hearings on the Regulation of Stock Exchanges Before the Senate Committee on Banking and Currency*, 63d Cong., 2d sess. (1914), 555–64.

2. Lawrence E. Mitchell, *The Speculation Economy: How Finance Triumphed Over Industry* (San Francisco: Berrett-Koehler, 2007), 236.
3. The Jones bill was H.R. 15399, 65th Cong., 3d sess., January 30, 1919. The Taylor bill was H.R. 15477, 65th Cong., 3d sess., January 30, 1919.
4. Lyle, "Senate Career of Carter Glass," 21–24.
5. Ralph F. de Bedts, *The New Deal's SEC: The Formative Years* (New York: Columbia University Press, 1964), 25.
6. Michael Parrish, *Securities Regulation and the New Deal* (New Haven, CT: Yale University Press), 43; and Moley, *First New Deal*, 307.
7. Moley, *First New Deal*, 309–10.
8. Joel Seligman, *The Transformation of Wall Street: A History of the Securities and Exchange Commission and Modern Corporate Finance* (New York: Aspen, 3d ed. 2003), 54.
9. "This Week," *New Republic*, 75, May 24, 1933, 29–30.
10. Seligman, *Transformation of Wall Street*, 66–67.
11. Ibid, 69.
12. Parrish, *Securities Regulation*, 114–15, n. 6; and Seligman, *Transformation of Wall Street*, 84.
13. Twentieth Century Fund, *Stock Market Control* (New York: D. Appleton-Century, 1934), 167; and S. 2642, 73d Cong., 2d sess., February 7, 1934.
14. Parrish, *Securities Regulation*, 115.
15. Joseph P. Kennedy, *I'm for Roosevelt* (New York: Reynal & Hitchcock, 1936), 94; and John Brooks, *Once in Golconda: A True Drama in Wall Street 1920–1938* (New York: Harper & Row, 1969), 203.
16. Joseph P. Lash, *Dealers and Dreamers: A New Look at the New Deal* (New York: Doubleday, 1988), 168.
17. "Roosevelt Wants 'Teeth' in Stock Exchange Bill: Seeks Speculation Limit," *New York Times*, March 27, 1934.

18. *Congressional Record,* 78, 73d Cong., 2d sess., April 30, 1934, 7693.
19. Parrish, *Securities Regulation,* 129.
20. John Thurston, "Politics and People," *Washington Post,* May 16, 1934.
21. de Bedts, *New Deal's SEC,* 71.
22. Seligman, *Transformation of Wall Street,* 99.
23. Koeniger, "Unreconstructed Rebel," 109.
24. Brooks, *Once in Golconda,* 201.
25. William O. Douglas, *Go East, Young Man: The Early Years: The Autobiography of William O. Douglas* (New York: Random House, 1974), 297.
26. James M. Landis, *The Administrative Process* (New Haven, CT: Yale University Press, 1938), 27.
27. SEC Historical Society, "431 Days: Joseph P. Kennedy and the Creation of the SEC (1934–35): The Kennedy Legacy: The Best New Deal Agency," www.sechistoricalsociety.org.
28. Matthew P. Fink, "The Strange Birth of the SEC," *Financial History,* 86 (Summer 2006), 16.

CHAPTER 9 NOTES

1. Marriner S. Eccles, *Beckoning Frontiers: Public and Personal Recollections* (New York: Alfred A. Knopf, 1966), 81.
2. Sydney Hyman, *Marriner S. Eccles: Private Entrepreneur and Public Servant* (Stanford, CA: Stanford Graduate School of Business, Stanford University, 1976), 155.
3. Burns, *American Banking Community,* 144.
4. Eccles, *Beckoning Frontiers,* 175.
5. Ibid, 197.
6. Walter Lippmann, *Interpretations 1933–1935* (New York: McMillan, 1936), 185; "'Minimum' Bank Law," *Business Week,* February 9, 1935, 8; and Burns, *American Banking Community,* 147.

7. Glass to Smoot, January 22, 1935, Box 283; Glass to M. B. Well-born, February 16, 1935, Box 304; Glass to Ralph Robey, March 13, 1935, Box 304; and Glass to Willis, April 3, 1935, Box 382, Glass MSS.
8. Burns, *American Banking Community*, 155–56.
9. Ibid, 160.
10. *Congressional Record*, 78, 74th Cong., 1st sess., April 29, 1935, 6512.
11. Burns, *American Banking Community*, 166.
12. Eccles, *Beckoning Frontiers*, 228–29.
13. Glass to Willis, January 22, 1930, Box 382, Glass MSS.
14. Glass to Thomas B. McAdams, August 27, 1935, Box 334; and Glass to Frederick E. Lee, December 1, 1935, Box 317, Glass MSS.
15. Koeniger, "Carter Glass," 133.
16. Eccles, *Beckoning Frontiers*, 221.
17. Lippman, *Interpretations*, 194; Burns, *American Banking Community*, 174–75; Allan H. Meltzer, *A History of the Federal Reserve, 1, 1913–1951* (Chicago: University of Chicago Press, 2003), 485–86; and Conti-Brown, *Power and Independence*, 30.
18. Glass to Robert L. Owen, September 23, 1938, Box 340; and Glass to Edmund Platt, November 29, 1938, Box 383, Glass MSS.
19. George William Dowrie, *Money and Banking* (New York: John Wiley, 1936), 500–501; "New Bill Will Let Banks Underwrite Securities Again," *New York Times*, June 23, 1935, 1; "Bank Bill Revision Out," *New York Times*, July 2, 1935, 1; and "Wall St. Bankers Split on Glass Bill," *New York Times*, July 6, 1935, 1.
20. Burns, *American Banking Community*, 170–71.
21. Ibid, 171.

CHAPTER 10 NOTES

1. Glass, *Adventure*, 240; and Willis, *Federal Reserve System*, 133–34, 41.

2. Robert H. Wiebe, *The Search for Order 1877–1920* (New York: Hill and Wang, 1967), 206.

3. Melvin I. Urofsky, *Louis D. Brandeis: A Life* (New York: Pantheon, 2009), 346.

4. Otis L. Graham, Jr., *An Encore for Reform: The Old Progressives and the New Deal* (London: Oxford University Press, 1967), 29.

5. Smith and Beasley, *Carter Glass,* 364.

6. William Lasser, *Benjamin V. Cohen: Architect of the New Deal* (New Haven, CT: Yale University Press, 2002), 327.

7. Glass to R. D. Gould, January 8, 1935, Box 337; and Glass to R. G. Leffingwell, July 12, 1933, Box 147, Glass MSS.

8. Alfred Lief, ed., *The Brandeis Guide to the Modern World* (Boston: Little Brown, 1941), 70.

9. Since 1950, Congress has enacted the Bank Holding Company Act of 1956, the Bank Merger Act of 1960, the Bank Merger Act of 1966, the Savings and Loan Holding Company Act of 1968, the Bank Holding Company Act of 1970, the Federal Credit Union Act of 1970, the Investment Company Amendments Act of 1970, the Securities Reform Act of 1975, the International Banking Act of 1978, the Depository Institutions Deregulation and Monetary Control Act of 1980, the Garn-St Germain Depository Institutions Act of 1982, the Competitive Equality Bank Act of 1987, the Financial Institutions Reform, Recovery and Enforcement Act of 1989, the Federal Deposit Insurance Corporation Act of 1991, the Riegel-Neil Interstate Banking and Branching Efficiency Act of 1994, the National Securities Act of 1996, the Gramm-Leach-Bliley Financial Services Modernization Act of 1999, the Sarbanes-Oxley Act of 2002, the Financial Services Regulatory Relief Act of 2006, the Federal Housing Finance Regulatory Reform Act of 2008, the Emergency Economic Stabilization Act of 2008, the American Recovery and Reinvestment Act of 2009, and the Dodd-Frank Wall Street Reform and Consumer Protection Act of 2010.

10. The Commodity Futures Trading Commission, the Comptroller of the Currency, the Consumer Financial Protection Bureau, the Federal Deposit Insurance Corporation, the Federal Housing Finance Agency, the Federal Reserve Board, the Financial Industry Regulatory Authority, the Financial Stability Oversight Council, the Municipal Securities Rulemaking Board, the National Credit Union Association, the National Futures Association, the Public Company Accounting Oversight Board, and the Securities and Exchange Commission.

11. Conti-Brown, *Power and Independence*, 258.

12. Edwards, *Evolution of Finance Capitalism*, 332.

13. Kevin McCoy, "Dodd-Frank Act: After 3 Years, A Long To-Do List," *USA Today*, September 12, 2013; and Mark Koba, "Dodd-Frank? More Like Dud-Frank for Lots of Folks," *CNBC.com* from http://www.cnbc.com, June 4, 2013.

14. Thomas A. Hoenig, speech, "Global Banking: A Failure of Structural Integrity," Institute of International and European Affairs, Dublin, Ireland, December 13, 2013.

15. Dylan Matthews, "Elizabeth Warren and John McCain Want Glass-Steagall Back. Should You?" *Wonkblog* from http://www.washingtonpost.com/blogs/wonkblog, July 12, 2013; Gretchen Morgenson, "Break Up the Bank? It's Not for You to Ask," *New York Times*, Sunday Business, March 2, 2014, 2; David M. Herzenhorn and Sewell Chan, "Financial Debate Renews Scrutiny on Banks' Size," *New York Times*, April 21, 2010; Simon Johnson and James Kwak, *13 Bankers: The Wall Street Takeover and the Next Financial Meltdown* (New York: Pantheon, 2010), 215, 216; and James R. Barth, Gerald Caprio, Jr., and Ross Levine, *Guardians of Finance: Making Regulators Work for Us* (Cambridge, MA: MIT Press, 2012), 215–232.

16. "The One Giant Left," *The Tulsa Tribune*, January 7, 1938.

17. Peter Norbeck to W. L. Baker, March 21, 1933, Box 1, Folder 3, Peter Norbeck Papers, University of South Dakota.

Index

Bank(er)s, commercial: and borrowing on U.S. government bonds, 70; and Carter Glass, 35, 59, 61, 63, 64, 68, 70, 99, 113, 114, 115, 167, 168, 169, 170; and Ferdinand Pecora committee, 109; and First Bank of the United States, 15; and Franklin D. Roosevelt, 103, 168; and Glass-Steagall Act of 1933, 118, 169, 170, amended to permit commercial banks to affiliate with securities firms, 174–75; and Louis D. Brandeis, 173; and Nelson W. Aldrich, 114; and Panic of 1907, 18, 19; and private investment, 80; and Pujo subcommittee, 29; and rediscount, 68; and securities activities, xiii, xiv, xv, 24, 73, 75, 76, 112, 114, 115, 139, 140, 141, 170, 175, 176; and securities affiliates, 73, 75, 76, 87–88; and securities speculation, xv; and state-chartered trust companies, 17–18; big city, 63; credit extended by, 61; Federal Reserve Banks' discount rates to, 66; involvement with speculative securities activities, 73, 75, 115; loans made by, 64, 65, to security firms, 76, to security affiliates, 76; New York, 65, 109, 113; oppose reforms, 83; personnel of, 114; separating from investment banks, xiv, 96, 113, 114, 118, 170, 173, from security affiliates, 76, 90, 112, 113, 114, 115, supported, 113; tying together, 16; underwriting securities, 167, 168. *See also* Bank security affiliates

Bank failures (Great Depression), 82, 102, 106

Bank holiday (March 1933), 113, 117; and Emergency Banking Act of 1933, 104–105; and Franklin D. Roosevelt, 125, uses Trading-with-the-Enemy Act to declare, 104, 123–24; and Herbert Hoover, 102–103, 104; Carter Glass opposes, 102, 105, 124, holds tongue over, 125; increases public demand for federal deposit insurance, 102; national, 101, 102–105; states declare own, 102, 103

Banking Act of 1935: and Carter Glass, 162, *163*, 164, 165, 166, behavior during battle over, 166–67, believes he triumphed over Eccles and Roosevelt Administration, 165, and commercial banks and securities, 167–68, what he won, 166, what he lost, 165–66, 166–67; and Federal Reserve Bank Governors, 164, 165; and Federal Reserve Board, 163, 164–65, 166, 167; and Federal Reserve System, 165, 166; and Open Market Committee, 155, 156, composition of, 163–64, 166; assessments of winners and losers in battle over, 165–66; Franklin Roosevelt creates new central banking model, 166, opposes Glass's commercial bank proposal, 167–68 signs, 162, *163*; House bill, 163; Marriner S. Eccles creates new central banking model, 166, suggestions for act, 155–58, 161, 162, 163–64, 165, 166, thinks he and Roosevelt Administration winners in act's provisions, 165, wins main point, 164; provisions of, 163–65; Roosevelt Administration's commitment to Eccles's program, 167. *See also* Omnibus Banking Bill of 1935

Banking bills. *See* Emergency Banking Act of 1933; Federal Reserve Act of 1913; Glass, Carter: *various entries*; Glass-Steagall Act of 1933; Omnibus Banking Bill of 1935

Banking Law Journal, 42

Bank notes, national, 15, 34